William Stephenson, PhD

A New Way To

Hope

STORIES THAT DESCRIBE THE JOURNEY TO HOPE

A New Way To Hope
Copyright © 2025 by William Stephenson, PhD

ISBN: 979-8993513423 (hc)
ISBN: 979-8993513409 (sc)
ISBN: 979-8993513416 (e)

William Stephenson Books
www.williamstephensonbooks.com
stephenson2789@gmail.com

Table Of Contents

Chapter One

Children

Chapter Two

Young Adults

Chapter Three

Adults

Chapter Four

Hope in Other Circumstances

Preface

When I decided to write a book about Hope, I realized that I had all the stories I needed. I knew the effort my patients had made to embrace this word we call Hope, and it needed to be told.

I returned to my progress notes, conducted countless phone interviews with family members, sent numerous emails and letters, and listened to hours of remembrances, all to get more information and permission to quote their loved ones and give more detail about the outcome of their loved one's battle with a life-threatening illness. This permission was essential if the person was a minor. I was successful in getting many releases, but there were several others that I could not get, and those cases were returned to my files.

I am convinced that no one should come to the end of life without hope. Those who must witness a loved one coming to the end of life should also not have to face that moment without hope. That has been the call in my practice as a therapist to the dying and their loved ones. Whether the patient was six or sixty, they deserved to embrace a profound hope.

For many, hope equals cure. Unfortunately, this is an equation that often positions a person with a life-threatening illness in a corner. What happens when that equation proves to be wrong? When one sits in front of their oncologist and is told that there is nothing more that they can do to cure this form of cancer, where is hope? To receive that kind of news destroys what most people understand as their foundation for hope.

I wrote these stories with a strong emphasis on recovery, the opportunity to experience life when death seems imminent. In each case, I attempted to get the client to discover what meant the most to them and then focus on that. What could they put into that which gave them meaning? Because therein would lie their hope. A hope that no one, no disease, could take away from them.

Some would even come to understand that there was no hope in the disease that was taking their life. But some would come to realize that what they put into this life gave them meaning, gave them purpose, gave them even hope. It is what I would come to call a Phenomenological Hope. A Hope that equals meaning and purpose.

The dying can be our teachers, no matter what their age. They would urge you to ask yourself what is important, and then they would say, "Now, *what is important to you **truly**?*" When you can answer that, then you are on your way to discovering a hope that can never be taken from you.

It is in the spirit of those who rediscovered a hope that would sustain them through their most difficult time in life that I have dedicated all of the proceeds from this book to **Rachel House**.

Their program is dedicated to women with children who are homeless and are in a violent relationship and women who have lost hope. Rachel House will help them rediscover a hope they can grasp to move forward in their lives. The purchase of each book will help bring hope to the most vulnerable women and children in the San Diego community.

Introduction

When You Do Not Know About Tomorrow

It seems appropriate to consider something common to us all in this COVID age: We don't know about tomorrow. Martin Luther cried: *"What's more miserable than uncertainty?"* [1]

Someone said that there are two things we all experience: Death and Taxes. The problem is that taxes get worse.

The fear of the unknown, death can surface significant anxiety and can cause great discomfort for ourselves and those around us.

Poet and Philosopher Soren Kierkegaard insisted that uncertainty is the source of anxiety. He said, *"Anxiety is the next day."* [2]

Anxiety is not knowing. Anxiety is living in the middle of a deadly virus. This element of uncertainty surrounds us. If we're going to experience genuine hope, we need to discover how to cope with this anxiety and uncertainty of a future filled with the unknown.

One of the ways people try to cope with anxiety and uncertainty is by gathering as many guarantees as possible, such as hundreds of rolls of toilet paper! But we found no easing of our stress with that.

Another way some people try to cope with uncertainty and discover any hope for tomorrow is by getting control of all that is around them. And what does that look like? All the bills will be paid, all of the children will be out of the house and happy with life, and all of our problems will be solved. Then we can relax and enjoy life. Even Jesus said that a person with a "tomorrow lifestyle" is a fool. Hoping for a secure tomorrow is an illusion.

There is reason to have anxiety around death. As one patient said to me, *"Death is the absence of life and everything that I know and care about."*

But there is more to it than that. For many, especially in this COVID world in which we live, there is the dying process. That may be the "elephant in the room" that sends our anxiety out of control. As one patient said to me, *"It's not death but dying that is such a drag. The constant waiting for the inevitable, the anticipation of the pain, constipation, the loss of dignity and privacy, bedsores, the loss of my libido, being unable to clean myself. It's all these little acts of dying I can't handle. Death can't be this bad."*

Where can genuine hope be realized while dying and death? That's what this book wants to answer. And there is more than one answer. But the journey to a realistic hope begins with the understanding that tomorrow is not promised, and thus, we must not be careless with today. Those who choose to find hope this way will no longer let anger, resentment, and grudges go on and on and on, convinced that tomorrow is already theirs.

When we accept the uncertainty of tomorrow, it energizes our confidence that today is a gift. Then our focus can become reconciling and forgiving and loving, not just to others but also to ourselves, and now.

There is a book by L.M. Goodman entitled *Death and the Creative Life*.[3] Dr. Goodman interviewed several famous artists and scientists, such as Alan Arkin, Isaac Stern, and several Nobel Peace Prize winners.

In the many questions she asked them about death and dying was this question: *"Do you think that if it were possible that we could do away with death, would it be a good thing?"*

Everyone interviewed said it would be the worst thing to happen to us. A realistic hope is found in the knowledge that we are going to die. It energizes us to be creative now.

Death is not some monkey wrench that God has thrown into the machinery of our lives. Instead, death is a purposeful part of God's providence. Knowing that this day is a gift, that tomorrow is not yet given or guaranteed, energizes us to live fully now. This is a hope that is humble and filled with gratitude. It's a hope that can build bonfires. It's a hope you will now read about that will perhaps urge you to modify your understanding of this four-letter word...Hope.

What you think, you become
What you feel, you attract
What you imagine, you create

—*Buddha*

CHAPTER ONE

Children

There was some risk in putting all the stories of the children into one chapter. They are clearly the most gripping testimonies of the way hope can happen for those with a terminal illness. I have discovered that the hope the children embraced was without prejudice, it was so genuine and authentic. It often came to them on a collision course with the enemy, the disease.

Children have a sense of hope that is nearly indestructible. They have this remarkable ability to embrace a hope that is to be exercised in the present, in the moment. It is not a hope for something in the future but something that they experience in the present. This is illustrated in the stories in this chapter.

"Bonfires" is the "signature" of this kind of hope. Anthony's hope was found in what he could do to make a "bonfire" take place.

Christal put her hope into all of the people that inspired her and cared for her.

Candace and James would not only care for one another when both were alive, but when only one was still alive the other continued to be there in spirit to the very end.

Then a story by Peter DeVries and his daughter.

Paul discovered his hope would give him the energy to reach out to children who were also very ill, and he would make a difference in their lives.

Then a different kind of story about a group of children. They had each lost a loved one in a senseless shooting in the city's community center. Their story, unfortunately, is one that is occurring too often in our society.

I hear from these children from time to time and they are still struggling when they recall witnessing their loved one being shot and killed right before their eyes.

Phillip. A child who hungered to be included and yet it would be his wisdom that inspired hope.

Followed by the poetic wisdom of Carrie.

The chapter concludes with two stories of teenagers. Paul, who gave so much of himself for others and would die surrounded by children, family, and staff. And Steven, who died alone but not without hope.

The hope these children modeled inspired my own. A hope that may not cure or solve but one that challenges me to stay involved even when hope seems so hidden.

The natural flights of the human mind
are not from pleasure to pleasure
but from hope to hope.

—*Samuel Johnson*

Hope is passion for what is possible.

—*Soren Kirkagaard*

Bonfires

Part I

His name was Anthony. He was nine years old and from Jersey Shores. He was a kid who loved the beach and sand so much that he practically lived there. But he had cancer. Bone cancer. Initially in the spine, it was spreading rapidly. He came to California to participate in an experimental trial, but his chances were not good. I was asked to be part of his care as a counselor to him and his family.

Anthony liked to draw. That was going to be my way of getting through to him. We started to draw together, almost competitively. But the rule I expected us to follow was to describe or explain what the drawing meant or how we felt about what we had drawn. We spent several hours drawing and talking about our drawings and our lives.

"Dr. Bill, what are you drawing today?"

"I'm drawing the house I grew up in. Would you like to see it?"

"Why did you draw this house today and not yesterday?"

"Anthony, your intuition is incredible. Because today is the day my father died, and I was home at the time I was told of his death. I drew the house today to remember him. Anthony, what would you draw that will help others remember you?"

He thought about this for several moments, then said, *"I would draw myself running on the beach like I used to before the cancer. I want people to remember me when I was well, not when I was sick."*

"Would you draw that for me, Anthony? I've only known you when you've been sick. Would you show me what you were like when you were well?"

"Sure! But would you tell me more about your father, Dr. Bill?"

"I will, but will you tell me more about how you feel about your battle with cancer? Would you be willing to draw me a picture of that?"

"Tomorrow, when you come to see me again, I will have a picture of me and my cancer."

"Fair enough. Now, let me tell you about my father."

He listened intently as I described my father's life and battle with a rare disease and how, as a fifteen-year-old, I made the commitment to care for him until his death. Anthony had many questions, and eventually, he began to understand that my relationship with my father was more important than dwelling upon his impending death. Death could never take away the love my father and I had for each other.

"Dr. Bill, I already have a drawing of me and my cancer. But I was afraid to show it to anyone. I think I can now." He pulled a picture out of his dresser drawer. I asked him to describe it to me.

"This is a picture of a rocket that is just about to crash into a fiery mass of destruction, hurting all those near it."

"I see five people nearby. Is that your mom, dad, and your sister? Who are the other two?"

"My grandparents."

"And the rocket is you, isn't it?"

"Yes. My cancer isn't just killing me, but it's destroying everyone near me. We were all so happy until I got cancer. It's all my fault!"

Then Anthony leaned against me and wept. And he wept. He hadn't cried like this ever before. He felt so responsible for all the sadness and anguish his family endured.

The next day, I called for a family conference, and I asked Anthony to share his picture. I told them no one was to leave, no matter how emotional things got to be, and it was indeed a very emotional time. But they listened to him, and Anthony felt they had listened. They talked about their journey with this disease that had attacked their son, her brother, and their grandson. They told the truth. For the first time, everyone was telling each other the truth.

It was a marathon session, and we would have more of them from time to time so they would stay committed to the honesty this nine-year-old said he needed from them.

The last drawing Anthony gave to me was a picture of the ocean with the sun on the horizon. It was a beautiful and colorful picture. And flying around in the sky were five birds all clustered together.

"Are the birds your family, Anthony? And is the sun setting a symbol of you?"

"Yes and no, Dr. Bill. You forget I'm from New Jersey, and, unlike here in California, the sun rises on the ocean's horizon."

"No more rockets crashing, huh, Anthony?"

"No more crashing rockets, Dr. Bill. I'm into sunrises."

Part II

"Anthony," I asked, *"you're going home to New Jersey tomorrow. Is there anything you want to talk about before you leave?"*

The trials did not work for Anthony, and he would be going home without a cure and what seemed to his family as if all hope was gone. Suddenly, everything seemed to be an ending, and they dreaded thinking of a new beginning without Anthony, their son, brother, and grandson.

"When I get home, I want to go to the beach. I know I can't get in the ocean or use my beach board, but I want to be out there so that I can watch my friends, smell the ocean air, and be a part of the action for as long as I can. Maybe even build a bonfire when the sun goes down. Do you think my parents would let me? I can't walk, but I could be carried, or maybe the lifeguards would help with their Jeep. I don't know, I was just thinking."

"Anthony, one way to convince them is to think beyond yourself. Who would you consider inviting to this event? Who would value being a part of this event with you?"

Together, we began to list everyone he wanted to invite. More than forty people ended up on his list.

"Now, Anthony, why do you want these particular people?"

"I want to thank them for their love and support since I got sick. I want to tell them how much they mean to me."

"Remember the song I taught you and your family to use to remind each other of your commitment to each other?"

"I could teach them that song, and then they would be part of that commitment! Yeah, that would be so cool!"

"Sounds like we need another family conference, Anthony. Are you up for that? And you need to prepare yourself if they don't support your idea." Remember, you've been thinking about this, but they haven't. You may have to give them some time to get on board. Are you okay with that?"

"I understand, Dr. Bill. But I'm running out of time."

A long silence lingered between us as we just looked at each other. Tears welled up in both of our eyes and a long hug followed. A family meeting took place soon after. Anthony presented his project in front of me after several rehearsals. They thought it was a great idea with conditions. His fever had to be low-grade. His pain had to be at a manageable level, and there had to be a controlled time of two hours. And the weather had to be user-friendly with low winds. He agreed. Anthony and his family left the next day. Their trip to California had come to an end. But their journey back to New Jersey had a new beginning.

Part III

Anthony went home and immediately started planning his beach event. He spent every waking hour when he was strong enough planning, writing invitations, and getting help from his friends, who now came over to visit with him because they felt so included in the planning. Occasionally, we would Face-Time his meetings about the Bonfire event with his friends and family. He kept me informed through every step of the progress. And, he expected me to somehow attend. I knew how many like Anthony I was committed to, and he understood that they needed me just as he had.

"Dr. Bill, it's really going to happen!" Everyone I've sent an invitation to wants to come! Did you get yours?"

"Yes, Anthony and I said I'd try to be there via FaceTime."

"Fantastic, Dr. Bill. I'm so excited! This has taken on a life of its own. I have so much hope that this is going to work. Thanks, Dr. Bill, for giving something to hope in."

"Are you ready to teach them the song, Anthony?"

"The family and I sing it every night before bedtime. I'm ready and printed it out so everyone will have the words."

The night of the bonfire was a perfect night. Anthony made his "grand entrance" via the lifeguards. All six jeeps in the caravan delivered Anthony with cheers and horns. More than sixty people attended, and they were all given an opportunity, if they chose, to share with Anthony and the others how important this event meant to them. I watched on FaceTime, but Anthony didn't know that I was a short distance from observing this wonderful celebration of life.

Then Anthony asked them to turn to the song sheet they had been given. It was time to close the bonfire celebration. Anthony told them that these words were from the Book of Ruth and were Ruth's covenant with her mother-in-law, Naomi. He told them that this was now the covenant he and his family had claimed as theirs, and he invited them to be part of their covenant.

As he was about to lead them in song, I began to sing from a distance as I moved toward the circle around the bonfire. He recognized my voice. *"Dr. Bill!"* and struggled to stand out of his chair. He joined me in singing as we embraced along with his family. We sang the song through and then invited everyone to join us.

> *Wherever you go, I shall go.*
> *Wherever you live, so shall I live.*
> *Your people will be my people,*
> *And your God will be my God, too. (Sung 2-3 times)*

It was a very sacred moment for all of us. This now ten-year-old boy had transformed us all with a new hope and a new beginning. Anthony would die just months later from an unexpected infection with his family all around his hospital bed. They also fulfilled Anthony's request to sing their song after he was gone.

Every year, around the date of his death, many of the people who attended the first bonfire gather at that same place, build a huge bonfire, remember the life of Anthony, and always close with the song that reminds them of their covenant with Anthony and each other.

When Anthony was told to go home after his medical trials, he felt as if all hope was gone. His life had come to an end. What he discovered was that the only thing coming to an end was the trip to California. When he went home to New Jersey, he found a new beginning. He had hope again. He had a reason to fight for every day he could steal from death.

An Infinite Hope

She was just twelve years old. Her name was Christal. I kept using a "y," but she insisted on the "i." I used to tease her about that. It was our way of finding something to smile about. She would then tell me my name should be with a "v" instead of a "ph." But I insisted on the "ph." Then, we would start thinking of other names we could play this game with.

She was dying. I would be the family therapist for the six short weeks I came to know them. Christal had Cystic Fibrosis, some retardation, and battled pneumonia regularly. It would kill her eventually.

Christal came from an impoverished family. They couldn't afford the expensive medical care she needed, including a therapist. I'm not cheap, but sometimes I am free. Her family ended up declaring bankruptcy and sold their house. All to give Christal the care they wanted for their daughter.

They are amazing parents.

Christal's main issue was she knew she would never make it to thirteen, to be a teenager. She wanted the symbol a teen represented versus what a child represented. She was grieving over what could not be, not what she was dealing with physically.

Christal was also feeling guilty because she knew the financial bind the family was in because of her illness. She worried that her parents would not be able to afford new oxygen tanks or breathing medicine.

One night, she asked me to come and sit with her because she was unable to get to sleep, and she was afraid she couldn't breathe if she fell asleep, even though she was on oxygen 24/7. In the dark, I sat, and together we breathed.

I asked her, *"Christal when you are in bed alone at night, how do you slow your breathing so you can go to sleep?"*

She said, *"I look out my window at all the stars. I start naming them after all the people who have helped and loved me. But I always run out of stars."* And we began to name the stars that night until she fell asleep. Her hope was infinite.

I had to go away for five days. It had been a planned family event, and I couldn't change it. Christal knew this was coming and even encouraged me to spend time with family. Christal assured me that she would still be here when I got back. I wasn't so confident. I called every day. She was declining, and by the time I got back, she was in ICU.

"Hi, Chrystal, with a 'y.'"

With great effort through her oxygen mask, she said, *"Hi, Dr. Stevenson, with a 'v.' I waited for you."*

With tears in my eyes, I said, *"I love you, Christal, with an 'i.'"*

"I love you, Dr. Stephenson, with a 'ph.'"

She would die later that night with her parents, grandparents, and myself in the background.

Early the following day, as her parents and I were having coffee together in the hospital cafe, they said, *"Dr. Stephenson, we have decided to take all of the memorial money and give it to the Cystic Fibrosis Foundation, and we also plan to be speakers to support this cause. We want other parents to know they are not alone."*

They were on their way. They were broke and deeply in debt, yet full of hope. I want to think it was an infinite hope.

***It is because of hope that you suffer.
It is through Hope that you'll change things.***

—Maxine Lugase

Hope Held Together - Candace

Children know what the real question is in life. Not what are you going to be when you grow up? But what are you going to do with death? Kittens die, rabbits, guppies and fish die. Grandparents die.

My belief in life after death has been evolutionary. At first, I believed in it because people told me to believe in it. Then, as a child in Sunday School, I was taught to believe in it. And then again, I believed in it because I so desperately needed to believe in it. Serving as a therapist for many children and young people who were struggling with a life-threatening illness gave me even more confidence that there was life after death. Two children particularly were my inspiration. James and Candace helped me come to understand the certainty of life after death. This is their story.

James and Candace were both nine-years-old when I was asked to become their counselor. Of course, this would include active support and attention to their parents, relatives, classmates, neighborhoods, and so on. They both lived near each other but had never met. Until they were both diagnosed with forms of cancer that could not be corrected. James and Candace were terminally ill.

What they had in common was that they each were the only child in their family. They were also very outgoing and vocal about their diagnosis. My job was to help them understand their prognosis. By the time I was brought on board, they had become seasoned players of the cancer game and they looked it. Neither had hair, both had physical changes due to the chemotherapy, and they had learned how few if any children who weren't stricken with cancer wanted to be acquainted with them.

Candace was especially hurt by the social isolation. She was often vulnerable to infection and often isolated to reduce the potential for infection.

"Candace, what is it that bothers you the most about your battle with cancer?" I asked.

"Sometimes I feel like I'm being punished for getting sick," she said. *"All the kids I used to play with and were my friends, no longer want to be around*

me. *They never invite me to their birthday parties or after-school events. It's like they're afraid that they'll get what I have if they come play with me. Or, they'll make me sicker if they have a cold or something. I feel like I'm being punished for being sick.*"

"*When you go into the clinic for treatment each week, is it the same there too?*" I asked.

"*Oh, no,*" she replied. "*At the clinic, it's like coming home. Everyone is glad to see each other, and we all seem to understand each other. It's the one place I feel I belong. James is my best friend. You know him. But there are times when I wish I was just a normal kid and playing soccer or gymnastics at the Y or being a part of a sleep-over. I want to feel normal.*"

"*Candace, can I make a suggestion?*"

"*Sure, Dr. Bill. Anything.*"

"*Would you consider going to your friends and telling them what you are dealing with each day instead of waiting for them to come to you? You have a very special gift that most children don't ever experience. You are facing a disease that may take your life. Help them to understand that it is not something to fear and that you have no intentions of sharing it with them.*"

"*Ha! Now that's funny! I just wish that what they have they'd give it to me! Do you think they'd listen?*"

"*Candace, you have the gift and ability to help your friends and classmates and even your Sunday School class come to know something about life that no one else can share. If you reach out to them, you are no longer thinking about what you don't have, but what you can contribute, and therein lies the power of your hope. Am I making any sense?*"

"*You're asking me to stop looking out the window, wishing I could be out there. Would you be able to help me with that?*" She asked.

I said, "*Let's talk to your parents about this and if they support it, you can be sure I'll be there to help.*"

"*As you had requested, we were listening over the two-way. We've never heard her talk so much. We had no idea that she was feeling so isolated because of her illness. It made my heart ache for her,*" said Candace's mother.

15

"*Dr. Stephenson, we've put so much energy into protecting Candace that we didn't realize how that caused her to feel so left out of life,*" said Candace's father. "*What can we do? What needs to be done?*" he added.

"*As I understand it, in addition to the clinic where she gets her care, Candace has three venues that she values. There are the kids in the neighborhood, the kids in her class, and the kids in her Sunday School class. There may be other areas but not as significant as these. I want to suggest that you, along with Candace, speak to the teachers of the classes and then go to the parents in the neighborhood and see if each of these areas would be willing to have a meeting with the kids, and the parents if they want, so that Candace could talk about her disease and her prognosis. To give her an opportunity to help them understand and perhaps help them be less anxious as they struggle with the changes that have taken her from them. If I can be of any assistance with any of these areas, I will be glad to participate.*"

"*We too have felt isolated,*" said Candace's dad. "*We look at the parents and teachers and they look at us with sympathy, but we don't know what to say to each other. What you are suggesting is that we take back what this disease has taken from us. What this disease has taken from them: Candace. We may not be able to beat this disease, but we can help others to know that if this ever happens to them, they can find hope in those who have been there before them.*"

"*Let's go talk to Candace,*" said her mom.

"*Candace, we understand what you want to do, and you have our full support. Let's find a way to do this together,*" said her dad. And tears filled all of our eyes. Candace and her parents had found a new way to define hope.

Candace died just six weeks after this conversation.

Hope lies in dreams, in imagination,
and in the courage
Of those who dare to make dreams into reality.

—Jonas Salk

Hope Held Together - James

James was also nine years old and his cancer was very advanced. He knew that there would not be any more drugs/chemotherapy, surgeries, or radiation. He had done them all, but his cancer could not be stopped. He went to the same clinic as Candace and they became best friends. Portions of his story were shared by his mother and primary caregiver. It takes place in the dawning moments in Seattle. James is looking out his bedroom window at the incessant rain we were having.

"Hey, Sport," his mom said, sticking her head out past the opened door, *"what's going on? It's a little early for you to be up. Something on your mind?"*

"It's Candace. She died without me being able to say good-bye. I know she wanted to say good-bye too. We talked about how this disease wasn't beatable and we were both dying. I couldn't even go to her funeral or memorial service, whichever, because of this horrible weather. It's just not fair, Mom." Tears quietly began to creep down his face and onto the windowsill. It was as if the day and James were in tears over Candace.

"James, I have an idea. Let's have our own memorial service for Candace. Right here, right now. What do you say?"

"Yeah, Mom, Candace would understand, and I would be honoring our promise that whoever died first the other would be at the service. Sure. Let's have a memorial service for Candace. So, what do we need to do?" asked James.

His mom said, *"Let's call Dr. Bill. Maybe he can help us and besides, he went to Candace's service so he can tell us all about it."*

James said, *"Let me call him. I call him all the time."*

Smiling, his mom said, *"I call him frequently as well. He doesn't have all the answers, but he sure does know all the questions."*

"I'll never forget the school program he and I put on. There were hundreds of people there. From the school, the community, even the Mayor. And the parents! That was an awesome evening. I was able to tell them not about dying, but about how I am going to live until I die. And then we went to the college and we did a talk there. And then at the health insurance convention so that

we could talk about the importance of medical care for the children who are homeless. The last six months have been the best I have ever had. People will remember me for the way I lived my life, not because I was dying. Dr. Bill gave me a way to handle this disease that no one else could."

"I'll be there in an hour," I said. *"Don't start without me."*

When I knocked on their door, both James and his mom were there to greet me. I could sense that they had an agenda that would need some care. Both of them had been in counseling together and individually several times. They had both come to terms with James' prognosis and they had learned the importance and power that being transparent with the outcome was critical to the depth of their relationship. James had come to talk about his dying with his mom, Leslie, and she had come to the place where she would let him talk about it. However, it hurt too deeply for her to share with him, but she was getting there.

"So, what's going on?" I asked.

Leslie answered, *"Because of the weather, we couldn't attend Candace's memorial service and we wanted to know if you could help us do a service here."*

"Dr. Bill, she was my best friend. Can you tell us how her service went?"

"It was incredible. Her family had wanted the service to be for family only. They wanted a small memorial service in the chapel, not the sanctuary. However, when we got to the church, there were hundreds of people standing in front of the doors to the sanctuary. As we were about to enter the chapel, everyone began to sing, 'Wherever You Go.'"

"Oh, mom, can we do that for my memorial service?" asked James.

Tears welled up in her eyes and she said calmly, *"Of course, James, I'll make a note of it."* She then looked at me incredulously.

I said, *"Several people participated in the service and there was also a video that Candace had made to be the closing part of the service. I brought a copy of it with me so that when you feel up to it, you can watch it. But not without Kleenex."*

"Thanks, Dr. Bill. Maybe before you leave today," said James. *"But what I hope I can do is help create my memorial service and would you help us?"*

"Sure, James. The first thing to remember is that while the memorial service is about you, the purpose of the service is to give care and comfort for those who are attending, especially your mom and grandparents."

"I think now, I understand," said James. *"What do we need to do?"*

With that, the three of us sat down and watched and listened to Candace's video. She had mentioned James specifically and thanked him for his friendship and the many talks they had about being critically ill versus those who didn't want to talk about it. We then created a sketch of a memorial service with her inspiration.

After an hour, James was tiring, and we would continue developing his service another day. But, as I was leaving, Leslie asked him a question that surprised me. It was a question that told me she was becoming more receptive to her son's remarkable acceptance of the limit of life he understood he had.

She asked James, *"Honey, what do you want me to do when you come to the end of your life?"*

I could see James absorbing her question and realizing that he and his mom were now on the same page.

"I'm not sure. But what I think I'd like to have, is when I go to the hospital for the last time, tell the ambulance driver to turn on his siren real loud so that Candace knows I'm coming!"

It's difficult to describe but the three of us had a new understanding of hope. A hope that would not be defeated. A hope that would sustain James and his mother in the difficult months ahead. James didn't get those sirens. He died at home with his mother, grandparents, and me at his bedside. His last words to me were, *"Take care of my mom, Dr. Bill."*

Hope to the very end. I believe in life after death because I keep falling in love with people again and again and they die.

A postscript to this story. After his funeral service at their church, his casket was carried by the hearse to the cemetery, preceded by a convoy of motorcycle police, all with their sirens blaring the entire way, so that Candace would know that James was on his way.

A dream is the hearer of new possibility,
the great hope.

—*Howard Thurman*

A Course In Hope

Latrelle was seventeen. He and his family lived in the Pacific Northwest. It was his doctor who recruited me to take Latrelle and his parents on as clients.

"Dr. Stephenson, I am familiar with your work with persons with a terminal illness, especially with young people. I have a patient that I hope will accept you as his therapist. He is aware of his situation, and I have told him about you. Except for myself, he has not had a lot of experience working with a White person, but I assured him that you would address that, and he could then determine if it could work. Will you take his case?"

His doctor would continue to explain his diagnosis as a rare form of Glioblastoma, a tumor in the base of his brain, and it was not curable. Latrelle had less than six months to live. Latrelle was a popular senior in high school. He would not live long enough to graduate. He was also confined to the safety of his home since he was so vulnerable to infection.

The initial conversations with Latrelle and his parents went very well and my request to meet with Latrelle alone (on Zoom and Facetime) was accepted. He and I hit it off quite well.

"Latrelle, how long have you been battling this disease?"

"Seven months, and I know I'm losing the battle."

"How do you know that?" I asked.

"My parents are always crying, the look on my doctor's face, and everyone pretending that everything's going to be okay, but I know. I'm taking all the meds, but the headaches have only worsened. And now you come into the picture. When is it that someone will tell me the truth? I don't think I've got time for fantasies."

"What has this battle taken from you, Latrelle?"

"I've lost all my friends. I'm a Senior, and I think my friends are avoiding me because they might "catch" something from me. I wish I could tell them that I'm safe to be around."

"Would you be willing to make a list of your concerns on the left side of a piece of paper and on the right side some ideas on how to address them? Will you do that?"

"I can and I will. For the first time, I feel like I'm doing something for myself."

A Meeting With Friends

Latrelle agreed to schedule a meeting on Zoom with all his friends. He made a list of everyone he hoped would be there and then emailed the invitation to them, including the Zoom link to attend. Nearly forty attended.

Before the meeting, Latrelle agreed to talk to them about his battle with cancer. I said to Latrelle, "Perhaps if they were able to hear from you directly, they might be willing to talk about their feelings about you and share their concerns about being a friend to someone who doesn't have long to live. "

When they were all together, I just let them talk to each other until I thought it was time to address the "elephant in the room." Latrelle began to explain to his friends what kind of cancer he had and that it couldn't be cured. He told them that it seemed as if everyone around him was tiptoeing and pretending as if everything was going to be okay.

He said, *"I know how serious my situation is, and it's hard to deal with when I'm alone with it. You are my friends, my classmates. I need your help. I don't want to do this alone."*

And I added, *"Facing a terminal illness doesn't mean a person has to be placed in solitary confinement. Latrelle can teach you more about a part of life that people rarely receive: Dying and loss. And you can return that opportunity by showing him what true friendship really is."*

Zoom was filled with silence. Then, someone said, *"I've got your back, Latrelle."* And similar comments began to ring out. Following that meeting, Latrelle would get frequent phone calls each day; others would come and watch a ball game on TV, and still others would come and do homework with him.

"Dr. Bill, you have brought back my friends, and all of them end up wanting to know more about my illness and how I cope, knowing that I don't have long to live. One of my friends is doing a term paper on my situation, and another interviewed me for the school newspaper. It's amazing what is happening."

I said, *"Well, while all that has been happening, I had a conversation with your high school Principal. Evidently, he was deeply moved by the article about you in the school newspaper. He has taken personal responsibility for conducting a special Commencement so that you can receive your high school diploma. Do you think you would be up for that to happen?"*

"Awesome! Yes! Dr. Bill, it's the one thing I thought my cancer took from me that I could never realize."

I said, *"It's going to take a couple of weeks to organize, and I am concerned about your ability to thrive in this. You and I both know that there has been a decline in your condition. But your Principal needs your help. You will be on Zoom, but everyone else will be in the school's auditorium. He wants to know who you want to invite besides your family."*

"I'll start making a list. When does he want it?"

"Yesterday," I answered.

"Got the message. I'll get this done as quickly as I can. Wow! Dr. Stephenson. Thanks."

It would take three weeks to put together this special Commencement. Getting all of his classmates robed during the off-season of graduation exercises was monumental. Not to mention all of the faculty. And when the general public heard about it, his office was deluged with requests to attend, including all of the media. The auditorium was now out on the football field.

The procession of faculty and dignitaries was amazing to witness. But Latrelle was dressed in his cap and gown, and I even wore mine. There were several speeches, but the one I recall the best was from Latrelle's class president.

He said, *"Latrelle, it is customary to receive a graduation gift. Latrelle, you are our graduation gift. Your courage and determination have inspired so many of us to without fear face life and dying. There is no curriculum to help us deal with that as we leave high school."*

"And now, your gift from us. We have created a special fund in your name to develop a support system here at the school for any student who may experience what you are going through. And so far, we have raised more than $11,000. We have also requested that a new class be established to teach us about how we can handle the losses we will face following graduation."

"Congratulations, Latrelle. You have inspired a new curriculum in our school."

And then it was Latrelle's turn to speak. I could tell he had very little stamina left, and he decided to shorten his speech significantly.

"Yes, I am dying, but you have all helped me to put more into living these past few months than all of the rest of my seventeen years. You have no idea how you gave me back my hope. Perhaps that can be the title of that new class: Hope."

Latrelle was exhausted, and two days later, he was hospitalized, and he would remain there for a short time before he died. But his legacy would live on. Hope would soon become a "learning experience" for all at his high school. It was a good death.

Hope is being able to see that there is light despite all the darkness.

—*Desmond Tutu*

From Fear to Hope

It was a phenomenon that was beginning to occur in this country. Random acts of violence. It was occurring in schools and public places. For no apparent understandable reason, a person would come on school grounds and begin killing people. This kind of violence created some very difficult emotional times for survivors and victims who recovered from this violence. It also took its toll on the community where this violence took place.

It was one such community that asked some of us who were trained in complicated grief and sudden loss to give some time to their community where they had experienced a mass shooting in a community center. Six people were killed, including the shooter and several others were wounded. I was asked to be a part of a team of therapists who came in and assisted and trained local therapists, teachers, clergy, social workers, and other professionals who were overwhelmed by the large number of people who felt immobilized by the incident. My specialty of assistance was working with children and the fear that seemed to be in control of their lives.

Many children who were in the community center that day witnessed the carnage that took place and were now prisoners of this violence. They didn't want to go to school, play with other kids, be out of sight of their parents, or go outside. Parents were sharing how they couldn't even go to the store without their children pleading with them not to leave for fear they would be killed. They would wake up in the middle of the night screaming from night terrors, and many could not sleep alone. Like a virus, these fears spread to other children until many children in the community became immobilized that this would happen again.

After spending a week listening and absorbing the issues many children were sharing, I chose seven children, ages 10-13, to join me in developing a group that would meet twice a day for five days. In the middle of that time, we would all meet in front of their parents, teachers, and friends in a nearby college auditorium for an open group session. Significant progress was made at that session, not only for the children but for those witnessing this session.

To the children in the circle on stage, I asked, *"You were all there in the center when the shooting took place. Can anyone describe what you saw?"*

At first, there was just silence in the group. There was an uncomfortable silence, even in the audience. Then, the sharing began with random comments.

"There was so much blood." "I saw people writhing in pain." "Everyone was running to get out." "Someone pushed me under a desk, and I just heard nothing but screaming and explosions."

"I miss my mom. He killed my mom." "I'm not supposed to talk about this." "I'm supposed to pretend that nothing happened, but it did, and I wish I could change that." "I'm getting scared again, just thinking back upon it."

I asked the children, *"How has this experience changed you?"* Again, there was this disturbing silence. But not with the audience. People were crying and consoling each other. Tension was building.

"I can't sleep." "I have horrible nightmares." "I worry that someone's going to kill us." "I feel sick in my stomach, and I don't want to eat." "I find myself shaking for no reason." "All I want to do is stay in my room." "I worry that my dad or my mom won't come home from work because someone shot them."

"Do any of you know who did this?" I asked. All of them shook their heads. Some were getting restless sitting in the circle.

"Have you ever seen a picture of the man who did this?" I asked.

"My parents won't let me watch or talk about the news. I'm supposed to pretend that it never happened. But it did. I'm just glad he's dead." Said the oldest in the group.

"I have a picture of the man who did this. May I share it with you?" The audience became restless, and the children could feel the anxiety that was beginning to be in the auditorium. But no one in the group objected to the picture. *"I will put this picture on the floor in the circle's center."* As I did so, some children turned away from the picture. But most of them just sat there, staring at the image of the man responsible for the nightmare they were going through.

"What are you feeling right now?" I asked. Again, a long pause ensued.

The oldest began. *"I want to KILL him!"* And others began to inquire. *"Is he in jail?" "Did he get arrested?" "Is he still alive?" "Does he have any brothers?"*

"No, you can't kill him because he's also dead," I said.

"Well, I want to stomp on him!" said the eldest. *"Yeah!"* said others, and all of the others agreed.

"Go ahead!" I said. He stood up, went over, and started to stomp on the picture and cry simultaneously. Others followed suit, and others started to come closer as if to help in the assault on the picture. People in the audience watched in pain as they saw the children attacking the picture.

After a few minutes, I assisted the children to return to their seats and comforted those visibly upset. I could tell that the audience wanted to rescue the children, but my associate assured them they would be okay.

Once some calm came into the circle, I asked, *"Can anyone share how they feel right now?"*

"I'm just so angry!" said one and then another.

"But, do you feel afraid?" I asked.

"He can't hurt us anymore." said another.

"You will always remember this horrible experience, but you don't have to let it control your life. Now, we have to find a way to make that anger constructive for you. We need to put that energy into our lives in a helpful way."

I turned to the eldest, who was still visibly agitated, and said, *"Lin, do you love your father?"*

"Yes. Very much." He said.

"Is he here today?" I asked.

"Yes."

"Lin, can you recall when you said to your father, 'I love you.'"

He paused for a moment and then he said, *"I honestly can't remember."*

"Do you want to know how to start letting go of that anger, Lin? Find your father and your mother. Tell them how you feel about them; as you are telling them, there will be no fear, anger, or hurt."

Lin jumped up and ran to the edge of the stage, and there, with tears in his eyes, his father reached out to him. They held each other for the longest time, and Lin looked up at his father and said, "Oh, Daddy, *I love you so much."* And together, they exited the auditorium.

I turned to the other children and looked at them for only a moment when one of them said, *"Can we?"*

I nodded, and they all went to the edge of the stage in mass, and there were their parents. They embraced and cried, and one of the parents looked up at me and said, *"You gave us back our children. We know now that hope has returned to us. Thank you."*

I turned to the rest of the people in the auditorium and said, *"Children cannot yet experience fear and anger simultaneously. Your job in this community is to start getting your children angry. Move them from the fear that keeps them imprisoned. Get them to feel the anger that must come. The emotion of anger is healthy. What they do with that anger needs to be monitored. And then channel that anger in ways that give them meaning and purpose, as these children now have. And then, hope abounds."*

Strength is what keeps you holding on…
Faith is what assures you that everything matters,
Hope is what keeps us moving on
When everything is going wrong.

—Unknown

An Empty Tomb of Hope

To illustrate how we are and remain children of God, no matter what we've done or didn't do, we are not written off and discarded as losers. That we are Easter people. The tomb is empty and that is the center of our hope. I could not find the source of this next story. But it was told to me and I'm sure it has many versions. This is the one I was given.

A young couple had a son named Phillip. He was eleven years old, and he was a child with Down's Syndrome. He could not go to a public school like most children because he could not keep up with them and, he was also highly susceptible to becoming ill from viruses and germs from other children. He would look out the window hoping that he could play with other children someday.

After a significant amount of couple's counseling, his parents decided to risk Phillip's "entombment" and safety and allow him to participate in a Sunday School class of other eleven-year-olds. The class was taught by a very creative young man who was very committed to these nine boys and girls. He immediately realized that the class was not letting Phillip assimilate into the group because of his Down's Syndrome. He was different, but Phillip didn't want to be different.

On Easter Sunday morning, this very creative Sunday school teacher gave each child a plastic Easter egg that they could open and put things inside. He told the children in the class to go out on the church grounds and find some symbol of Easter and put it in their Easter egg, bring it back to the classroom, and there they would share what they had found.

When the children returned it was time for show-and-tell. One had a flower in it and the children cheered. Another had a butterfly and they oohed and ahhed. The teacher then came to an egg, and when he opened it up, it was empty. The class reacted with, "Oh, how stupid." "Someone didn't do it right." The teacher felt a tug on his sleeve, and it was Phillip and he said, *"That's my egg and I did do it right. The tomb is empty."*

An incredible silence fell over the class. A miracle came to that classroom that day. The children began to look at Phillip in a new way.

The children began to accept him. They let him be a part of the group, and suddenly Phillip was released from his tomb.

Later that summer, little Phillip died from complications of chickenpox! At his funeral, eight children marched together to his casket, and instead of putting flowers in his casket, to cover up the death, the class, along with their teacher, marched to the front of the sanctuary and placed an empty plastic egg to symbolize that Phillip was freed from his tomb.

But that empty plastic egg also freed Phillip's classmates from their tomb. They had learned that the next Phillip to join their class would be welcomed and feel included. Hope abounds.

Time is no longer endless
Or the horizon destitute of hope.

—*Charles Lindbergh*

How Hope Begins

Carrie was thirteen and a gifted writer. She shares in the poem the hope she would hang onto, as well as would hang on to her, in the strength and confidence she had in her mother. This is her remembrance of her initial journey with cancer.

The look in my mom's eyes
as I sat on the floor.
I squeezed my mom's hand
because I had no idea
what was in store.

My mom looked at me and said,
"Listen, baby, I've got something to say.
Just hold my hand tight.
Everything will be okay."

She said,
"Now, what I'm about to say
isn't as bad as it sounds,
but your lung infection
is more than profound."

I still didn't get it.
I didn't know what to say.
Nothing could hit me harder
than when she said CANCER
had come my way.

Hope springs eternal.

Hope Restored

The beginning of this story takes place in a children's cancer ward. One particular room was a sixteen-year-old boy diagnosed with cancer. He had just come out of surgery to amputate his left leg. Needless to say, he was in deep depression, and no one had been able to get him to talk about the surgery or anything else for that matter.

He had shut himself off from the rest of the world. Even his mother couldn't reach him. He became my next patient.

I sat down beside his bed and introduced myself. *"Paul, my name is Dr. Bill Stephenson, and I'm a counselor. I work only with kids like you who are facing a life-threatening illness. I know I can help you get through this, but only if you want to get through this. At least think about it, and I'll check in on you tomorrow. Okay?"*

Paul just looked up at the ceiling with no emotion shown. I got up and met his mom standing in the hallway.

"Dr. Stephenson, I am at my wit's end. He won't even speak to me, and he knows how hurt I am."

"He's here for a while," I said. *"Let's see if we can pull him out of his shell."*

Later that day, all the children in the ward (except infants) were to go to the recreation room to welcome Santa Claus, and I was to tell or read a story. Paul was also there in a wheelchair. I sat down on the area rug with all the children around me. As I was reading a story to the children, I noticed how much Paul was attentive. He wasn't in some other world. He was present the entire time.

Later that evening, his mother and I sat in his room, talking, but often distracted with the constant crying of the young child, whose mother had not been there the entire day. Finally, Paul's mother couldn't take it any longer. She burst out of her chair, went over to the young boy, and picked him up, walked over to Paul's bedside, and said, *"Here, Paul, you're not doing anything except feeling sorry for yourself. Hold the boy and help him to calm down."*

She placed the child in Paul's arms and stomped out of the room. I watched Paul and the young child for several minutes. Paul was so tender and caring. He looked at me, and I could see a little smile beginning to unfold. The little boy stopped crying. I returned the little boy to his crib, and Paul began to talk for the first time.

"I had been invited by a girl in my junior class to be her date to the annual spring formal. After my surgery, she sent me an e-mail saying that she had changed her mind and I would understand," he said bitterly. *"I understood. I mean who would want to go to the annual formal with a cripple? I feel like I don't belong anywhere. Except for tonight. Tonight, I felt like this is the only place where I feel like I belong."*

"Paul, you have gone through a tremendous ordeal, and I think you know that there is probably more to come. Your cancer is a tough one. It stands to reason that here you feel safe, and that's why a lot of the kids here consider this a part of their home because here their friends know what they're going through, and they want to support them like they get support."

"You know, Paul, you will be getting well enough to go home soon. Have you thought about what you want to do when you go home?"

"Tonight got me thinking. When Mom gave me the baby to hold and he quieted down, and watching you read stories got me to thinking. Dr. Stephenson, I could do that. Could I come back and volunteer here and read books to the children? Maybe I could help some teenager get past the shock of the word cancer, which I remember was like a kick in the stomach. Maybe I can help out around here. Or am I too young to volunteer?"

"I think you may have hit on something that a number of us have talked about. Peer support groups and teams. You would need to go through some training, but, Paul, yeah, I think you would be a terrific volunteer. Let me make some calls and see if we can get it arranged."

"Thanks, Dr. Bill. That's what most of the kids here call you. Is that okay?"

"Paul, I'm just glad you are talking again. I think you're on your way back from under that dark cloud."

"Dr. Bill, you gave me a reason to want to live again. You gave me back my hope."

Paul would get the training, and he came back to be the best reader we could ask for. He always found a way to turn each story into an adventure. When he came into the ward, every kid was out of their bed and following him around or waiting in the recreation room for him to come and read to them.

Six months would pass. Paul's condition worsened rapidly and an infection would be his downfall. When he entered the children's ward for the last time, he was in great pain, weak, and unable to get out of bed. But the kids kept sneaking into his room, asking him if he would read to them. He read to them until he could no longer. One night, a divine hope descended upon him, and he was gone.

Paul thought that his life was at an end when they amputated his leg. In a sense, it did come to an end, but he found a new life, a new beginning, and he came to live it passionately to the very end.

Courage is like love;
it must have hope for nourishment.

—*Napoleon Bonaparte*

Where Can I Go?

Steven was seventeen and battling fourth stage cancer. He was the only child of two parents who placed Steven in a war zone. Steven was in a lot of pain. Physically, emotionally, relationally. His parents were regularly yelling and screaming at each other, day and night. Steven's pain was so overwhelming that he often was self-administering his pain medications because he didn't want his parents to come into what he called his "bomb shelter."

His primary doctor had been treating Steven for two years and because he sensed that something was deeply troubling Steven, he asked me to consider being his therapist and send the bill to him. He also contacted Steven's parents and asked if I could come and see him and they agreed.

Steven's condition was clearly in the advanced stage. He would be one of several clients that fit into new criteria I was using to receive clients. I would now receive clients only if they had two months or less to live.

After we went through the usual assessment interview, I asked Steven, *"You and your doctor have had a conversation that was more than medical that moved him to call me and also have some conversation. Steven, I know we have only just met, but I also know that you are running out of time to have a purposeful conversation. Would you be willing to fill me in?"*

He stared out his window and then said without any emotion, *"I'm really jammed up and I don't know what to do about it. I have to get out of here, but I don't know where I can go. And even if I did know where to go, I couldn't do it. I just don't want to live like this any longer. I also don't want to die like this either. But there's nothing I can do about it. It is what it is. I'm probably just wasting your time."*

I waited without responding for a couple of minutes. Suddenly, I heard his mother scream, *"Screw you!"*

And then his father, *"Nooooo, screw you, jerk!"*

It was then that Steven's comment began to make sense.

I said, *"This goes on all the time, doesn't it."*

"Day and night, 24/7," replied Steven. *"And then they come in here and they're all so sweet and nice. As if nothing has happened. As if my hearing is incapable of functioning. Dr. Bill, I don't know how many times I have heard them scream at each other, 'As soon as he's dead, I'm out of here!' Followed by, 'Good riddance. It couldn't come sooner!'"*

"Dr. Bill, I feel like I'm homeless! If it weren't for my doctor and now, maybe you, I have no one I feel safe with."

"Then," I said, *"you need to understand what I'm about to say. What you shared with me stops right here. What you share with me will remain completely confidential. I will not be going from here to your parents and describe to them what occurred here. Do you understand what I'm saying?"*

"Anything?" he questioned.

"Anything," I answered.

"Having said that," I added, *"I want to suggest you consider giving me permission to discuss your case with your primary doctor. He's one of your biggest fans, Steven, and he has a deep concern for your welfare and I think he would be an even better physician for you if we kept him current with where you are emotionally with not only your cancer but also your home-life."*

"Dr. Bill," said Steve, *"I don't have a home. I live in a prison with two adults who are in this prison as well. My death will be the key that will unlock our prison doors. No, Dr. Bill, I have no home and I have no hope for a home."*

"Steven, would you consider changing your definition of the place we call 'home'?"

"Why? It's just a place where you live. Is it different?"

"Steven, it's time for me to go. Would you allow me to come back tomorrow?"

"I hope you will, but I get the feeling you're going to give me homework."

"I'm going to wait for you to say, 'pardon the pun.' That's exactly what you are to do. When you think of 'home' what words would you use to describe it without describing a physical building? What do you not have now that you want to have to get you through this last chapter of your life? Yes, Steven, this is the last chapter. Define what home can be for you within the limits you are given and let's see if it can happen. Because if it's possible, I'm going to find

a way for you to know and experience 'home.' Do you understand, Steven? I may fail but I don't think so. Help me to know what you mean by 'home' and then let's get to work to make some or all of that to happen."

"Wow! You sure get passionate about a four-letter word! Home, that is. Okay! I'll do the homework, so to speak. You're asking me to take on a task that pushes me to be truthful and honest instead of pretending, like I do most every day around here."

"I'm asking you to take you seriously. I do. Your doctor does. Together we may all learn something. Do you think that's possible, Steven?"

"I already have, Dr. Bill. You've also helped me to own another four-letter word."

"Really? And what might that be, Steven?"

Together, we said, *"Hope."*

Steven and I would meet nearly every day. Seeing a client that often has its risks. I had a team that helped to avoid many of them. My music therapist came regularly to work with him. He fell in love with her. I had a "spiritualist" who taught Steven about "centering" and meditation and the art of breathing that will touch your soul. Steven and I would journal and he discovered that what he wrote would still be here when he was gone. He had so much to say to those he would leave behind. My job was to help him write so that they would read it without judgment.

When I knew he was coming close to the end his doctor and I conspired.

"Steven, what do you need?"

"Dr. Bill, you have given me a sense of what it means to have a home. You, your staff, my doctor and his staff. You are the family I needed. But this place is still a living hell."

"Steven, your doctor and I have a plan. We want to suggest you come into the hospital and let you live out what it means to you to be home. A place of peace, a place committed to healing and caring. A place where you are safe. Your hospice care-taker can continue to give you basic care. Your doctor has been able to persuade your medical insurance carrier that you need immediate hospitalization. So what do you say? Are you ready to get out of here?"

"Dr. Bill, do you realize what you have done? Before I knew you, all I wanted to do was die. But now, I want to live as long as I can. Every day, you bring me someone or something that pushes me to want to live. And now, I get to die in a place where I can live until I die. Thanks, Bill."

"Dr. Bill, Steven. Remember?"

"I know. Boundaries."

Together we smiled followed by a hug.

Steven was admitted to the hospital three days later. I was shocked to see how fast the cancer was taking over. His lungs were full and breathing, let alone talking, became a challenge. His parents came with him and dramatically doted over him. But then they left. Incredible. They left!

I had been given permission to work with the nursing and support staff to understand that Steven was coming "home." They were to be his home until his death. They were to call him Steven whenever they could. Even the cleaning lady, and food server, and the security guard were to acknowledge Steven. To say, *"Good morning, Steven." "Good night, Steven."*

When Steven came into the area where his room was located, nearly every staff person came up to him and introduced themselves and welcomed him. *"Glad you're here, Steven."* And one of them even said, *"Welcome home, Steven. Welcome home."*

I decided to spend the nights with Steven. His parents usually left by six and the hospital wing was beginning to wind down. It got quieter, softer, like home. Steven and I would talk for just a few minutes at a time. It was all he could do.

"It's soon isn't it, Steven."

"Yes. I'm ready for the next journey. It's crazy, but I'm not afraid. I feel safe now. Thanks, Dr. Bill. And thank all of your staff. That music therapist is gorgeous."

"My God, you are seventeen aren't you. Way to go Steven. I'll be sure to tell her that you loved her flirtatious music." I caught him smiling for just a moment.

"Sleep, Steven. I'm going home and shower. I'll be back in a few hours."

I went home and showered and changed. I sat down and journaled. I fell asleep. I suddenly woke up as if someone was trying to wake me. I had slept for more than three hours. I leaped up and quickly drove to the hospital. I came into Steven's wing and the doctor on call was coming out of Steven's room. I knew why he was there.

He said, *"He went quietly. He died when no one was around."*

"That's Steven," I said. *"He wanted to do this alone."*

I know this will be difficult for some who have read this, but I believe that Steven had found hope again. I believe this because he gave me so much hope. Hope, like love, can only be given by those who have it to give.

CHAPTER TWO

Young Adults

As I engaged some clients who could no longer put their understanding of hope to cure, there came a point where there was no hope. It seems that a sense of hopelessness had to be experienced for hope to be re-experienced. While many of the stories in this book reflect that sense of hopelessness, the stories selected for this chapter illustrate it most clearly. It is a chapter dedicated to young adults as they tried to understand how their lives were ending, just as they were beginning to discover the joy of celebrating their freedom.

Yet, the stories selected are very different from each other. Jennifer, an impulsive twenty-three-year-old who learns the art of humility and letting her life be in God's hands. Carolyn and Alan is a love story and their hope is found in their relationship. The story of Bill, an AIDS patient is quite the opposite. He had no relationships and he found hope again.

The next story that follows should probably be left out of this book. I tried and was also advised to leave it out. I re-live this case on occasion and it still wakes me up in a cold sweat. I have this case separated from the others. I continue to ask myself, even after all these years, *"What could I have done differently?"* Thus, the title of the story: A Teachable Moment.

Lastly, the story of the one client that touched my heart and someone I think about often. Kathy. Someone who learned to reach out to others and found meaning. She found hope.

At the moment of death
I hope to be surprised.

—*Ivan Illich*

Finding a Hope That Works

It isn't easy for someone to shift their understanding of hope into a place they've never been to before. So many people spend their lives putting their hope in where they will have a solution to their problems. It's what I call a "fix-it hope." "I will place all of my hope in you if you can fix the problem I have." For a person who is facing a life-threatening illness or a parent whose child is facing a life-threatening illness, they are going to likely put their hope into anything or anyone that can fix their crisis.

When that hope fails them, to expect them to change their understanding of hope is as terrifying as being on a trapeze swing high in the air, with no net below, and then have to blindly let go, turn, and be caught by the other trapeze artist that they hope is there at the right time. That kind of hope is too risky. Better to lower your standards for having any hope at all. But it can happen.

Jennifer was just twenty-three and battling Leukemia. She was in the hospital because she was out of remission and losing blood. Suddenly, she gasped and lost consciousness, and began hemorrhaging. They rushed her into surgery to stop the bleeding, but the monitors were flat-lined. Miraculously, the surgery would give her another chance.

She recalled that episode to me. She said, *"There were five doctors standing over me. Each one of them working feverishly to keep me from dying. I knew I was indeed very near death."*

Then, she said, she began to pray. A prayer we must all say when we are having to let go of the old, not knowing what the new life will be like. She prayed, *"God, I let go, and I turn my life all over to you now. I am letting go, and I turn it all over to you."*

I call this the trapeze prayer and it's a prayer we must pray often. For one to experience a hope that will work, we must be ready to pray, *"God, I turn my life all over to you. I let go."* And, with blind hope, you turn to find yourself in the arms of a God who not only is our Creator but also our re-creator, again and again and again.

No one should die without hope. To be with someone who has lost all hope is a sacred time. It is a very intimate moment with someone. They feel like there is no place to turn: *"There is no cure for this disease. No cure. No hope. I just want to die."*

To bid that person to discover a hope that works is not an easy task. It's as difficult as standing outside the tomb of Lazarus and saying, *"Come out. Whatever it is that keeps you from embracing a new hope, let it go. Come out of your tomb."* But, be prepared to say it to them more than once. Often those whose hope has betrayed them are hard of hearing.

Hope itself is like a star –
not to be seen in the sunshine of prosperity,
And only to be discovered in the night of adversity.

—*Charles Spurgeon*

An Amazing Grace

He was twenty-nine and on top of the world. He had just finished his second Master's Degree in Psychology and was well on his way to getting his Ph.D. He had been offered an internship at a facility where he could get the two thousand hours and qualify to take the tests for licensure. It was an exciting moment in his life.

Then everything fell apart. He was attending a conference in Los Angeles, despite not feeling well, and he had a fever. In a break from the conference, he collapsed and was rushed to the hospital. After three days of recovery and testing, he would hear the word that would change his hopes and dreams for the next two years: Leukemia. He would lose his residency, the anticipated income, and a marriage, to name just a few.

He was not a model patient. He refused to accept the diagnosis until he hemorrhaged. Even then he resisted the horrible chemotherapy and radiation. At his worst, he had lost his hair, he could barely walk, and he weighed 127 pounds. He was a skeleton with skin. He would end up spending every cent he had, and borrowing more, to fight this invader of his life. He lost all hope of fulfilling his dream of becoming a psychotherapist.

He was accepted into a clinical trial for bone marrow transplantation. He was the oldest of ten patients in the trial. The second oldest was a young man who was married and a minister in a local church, Dan. They quickly became friends. They had the same doctor and went to the same clinic for treatment. They scheduled their chemo-therapy treatment at the same time and, out of spite, before getting their chemo, they would go have a huge Mexican breakfast which they would throw up following the taking of the chemo. Children.

Throughout this period of his life, he was in counseling each week. It was required to be in the trial. He would be the only one in the group to get a remission. His brother's bone marrow was a perfect match. The other nine would succumb to this once deadly disease.

When his friend, Dan, died, my client was in a deep state of grief and depression. But Dan's wife asked my client if he would speak at the graveside service that followed his funeral.

He said, *"My grief was dark and deep. My faith had died with him. At his gravesite, I felt helpless to say anything."* He said, *"I was too weak to even stand up, let alone speak. In the cemetery that day, I was needing someone to bring me a word, any word of hope. I begged God to give me a sign that would give his wife, as well as myself some comfort. Some hope."*

"And then," he said, *"hope came. Somewhere in the distance, came the sound of a bagpipe, playing Amazing Grace. When the song ended, there was a calm silence. He said to Dan's family that the words to that song would speak for us all. Words were unnecessary."*

My client, when everyone had left the gravesite, went and laid down next to the casket to have some time to say goodbye to his dear friend, Dan. As he was lying there, he heard the sound of someone nearby. He looked up and there standing over him was the piper. He said apologetically, *"I hope my playing didn't interrupt your service. I was just practicing."*

My client shared that the piper would never know that his "practicing" would save a wretch like him. Hope had been found in the least-likeliest of places. A cemetery. It was an amazing grace.

Hope is the only thing stronger than fear.

—*Robert Ludlum*

Hope Eternal

Part One

It was love at first sight. That's the only way I can describe it. Carolyn was just sixteen. She had an advanced form of cancer that was weakening her more every day. She was from South Carolina. She was accompanied by her parents who were very protective of Carolyn.

Alan was twenty-three and from New York City. He too had an advanced form of cancer and was in great pain. Alan had no one who accompanied him. He was on his own.

They had both come to try an experimental drug treatment program but their attempt to get some positive outcomes was not going to be achieved. However, they were too sick to discharge. They were both facing a terminal diagnosis and they knew it. Both were Christians. Alan, though, was much more skeptical, and Carolyn was evangelical with her faith.

I was assigned to prepare them emotionally for discharge as well as equipping them with a different kind of hope. A hope that did not include a cure. They were both so vulnerable, scared, depressed. As Alan once said to me, *"I wake up in the morning and the first thing I think about is that I have cancer and it's killing me. When I go to bed at night, the last thing I think about is that I have cancer and it's killing me. Dr. Bill, there seems to be no escape. It's so consuming."*

And then they met. Quite by accident, really. Well, almost by accident. Both in wheelchairs, Alan was going pretty fast down the hospital corridor when all of a sudden, Carolyn wheels out of her room, right in the middle of the hall, and nearly collides with Alan's wheelchair.

"Have you got a license for that thing?" she asked, sarcastically but with a smile all over her face.

"Sorry about that," he said sheepishly. *"It's just that it gets so tiresome just sitting around and waiting for news that is never good,"* said Alan.

"You, too, huh?" said Carolyn.

"What do you mean by that? You mean......" said Alan.

"We came out here from South Carolina to get good news and all we've gotten so far is bad news," added Carolyn.

There was a long pause as they just looked at each other. And then, *"Hi, Carolyn, I'm Alan and I'm from New York."*

"You know my name?"

"I asked around. You're the Princess of this floor. You are gorgeous. Sorry for being so forward but I don't have time to wait for the appropriate moment."

Another long pause as they looked at each other.

"Alan, you need to get a helmet on if you're going to race through these halls. And a horn." Then she started wheeling past him and down the hall.

"Where ya goin'?" asked Alan.

"To the veranda to watch the sunset."

"Can I join you?"

"No wheelies, Alan."

"No wheelies, it shall be, Carolyn."

Hope Eternal

Part Two

Down the hallway they went. Together. A new kind of hope began to emerge for both of them. In fact, those two wheelchairs were nearly inseparable to the end. They ate together, which was often just taking their medications, and spent long hours in the patients' lounge. They would talk and when they weren't talking, they would just sit and look at each other or doze in their chairs together. They would spend long hours at the end of the hall looking out of windows that displayed a beautiful ocean and sunsets.

I would see them for individual counseling nearly every day. But I couldn't get them to talk to me about their cancer. All they wanted to talk about was each other. Him or her! Alan said to me in one of our sessions, *"Before I go to sleep and when I come awake, the last and first thing I think about is not the cancer, but Carolyn."*

They were deliriously happy, and both felt deeply for the other, which included a deep spiritual connection. They could both sense what the other was thinking, feeling, hoping. Consistently, they would tell me what the other was thinking.

Carolyn's parents were struggling with this relationship. They wanted Carolyn to be happy in the midst of the peril she was facing. But they also didn't want her to possibly endure the feelings that might come should the relationship come to an end. They wanted to protect her from the pain and emotional upheaval that a "Dear John" love letter could bring. They worried that if, and more likely when the relationship ended, she would be greatly weakened by it. Thus, her parents asked me to hold a special counseling session.

"We are concerned, Carolyn. You spend ninety percent of your time with Alan. We need some of your time, too. We're losing you but there are times when we feel we've already lost you" said her dad. Her mom began to cry. No verbal communication took place for several minutes as Carolyn took hold of their hands and held them in hers.

And then Carolyn broke the silence. *"Mom, Dad, I never thought I would ever know love as I have witnessed you two know love for each other. Alan has given me a chance to get just a sense of what it must be like to love and be loved as deeply as you two do."*

She said in the most tender of voice, *"But we will never make love to each other. We will never have a wedding. Daddy, I will never realize a life-long dream of you escorting me down the aisle and into the waiting arms of Alan. And I will never be able to bear you grandchildren."*

Then, she said to her parents one final thing. *"Mom, Dad, because we believe our love is so genuine and sincere that God is with us, for us, and believes in us. We ask for your blessing. We ask you and invite you to share in our joy."*

Her father rushed and knelt in front of Carolyn, looked up at her, and, with tears flooding his eyes, said, *"Carolyn, we give you two our blessing and pray that whatever time you two have left, that it will be filled with tears, laughter, and love. Alan is and has always been the man I wanted to give my daughter's hand in marriage."*

I brought Alan into the meeting so that we could affirm the covenant that had just been made. They spent several minutes sharing their stories and pledging loyalty to the well-being of Carolyn, to him, and to their coupleness.

Hope Eternal

Part Three

Because there was no more medical intervention, they chose to find within themselves, and their faith, a journey at the end that was unique to this couple. Because they were no longer taking medications related to fighting cancer we managed to get them to be together in adjoining rooms. Carolyn's cancer was more profound. But the only medication they were taking was for the pain. Water and glycerin swabs for comfort in the mouth were the only other forms of medication.

They remained in this state for five days. They became the talk of the hospital. Two lovers, coming to the end of life with a passion of hope they had built together. Each only interested in the welfare of the other.

Carolyn said to me, *"Is Alan taking his pain medication? Is he still able to take it orally? If he can still hear you, tell him that I'm not going to be awake much longer. I'm so tired and my time is soon. I know it's soon for him as well. Dr. Bill, he has no one but you and us. I don't want him to die alone. Tell him that I will be waiting for him on the other side."*

I placed my cheek against hers and said good-bye. I went next door and found Alan barely conscious. But he said, *"I'm on my way, Dr. Bill. I don't even feel like I'm even here anymore. Tell C. that I will be waiting for her with open arms on the other side. Go. Dr. Bill. I want to be alone. I want to be with C."*

I placed my hand over his heart, and he knew it was my way of saying goodbye. I went back to Carolyn's room and her parents were in tears. Carolyn had just died. I stayed with them for a while and then went back to Alan's room. The nurses were all around him. The doctor had just pronounced Alan's time of death, just short of Carolyn's by one minute.

These two young people had learned to live life close and together. I remain convinced that they were so close and together in life, that they were able to plan death and life after death. They were able to orchestrate death so that they would go out together.

I was privileged to witness two people who were so deeply in love with each other that they could discover a hope that could be known by others I came to witness. A hope that was an eternal hope. A Hope Eternal. Indeed.

Faith is unseen but felt.
Faith is strength when we feel we have none.
Faith is hope when all seems lost.

—*Catherine Phillips*

Holding on to Hope

In the late 1990s, the AIDS epidemic was at its height and it was out of control because there was no apparent cure. It was killing young and old. At first, it was largely a gay issue but then it became an issue in the drug community. I had many clients who were young and working hard to have a promising future and then were struck down with this hideous disease.

One of these was Bill. When he became my client, so much had happened to him. Before he contracted AIDS, Bill was just twenty-seven years old. He was single, smart, attractive, and educated. He was active in his church and admired for his commitment. He taught the high school Sunday School class, a frequent liturgist, a member of the church board, and often volunteered to visit shut-ins and those in nursing homes. People would often invite him to their home for dinner.

But Bill had a dual life. In addition to all of the above, Bill struggled with Major Depression and had chosen to self-medicate with cocaine and heroin. It was in sharing a needle with someone he mistakenly trusted that gave him a new journey with AIDS and his life changed quickly and dramatically.

He lost a significant amount of weight and he looked like he was physically unable to give himself to any of his passions. When the church found out that he had AIDS they responded as many did at that time, they acted out of fear and ignorance. He was asked to stop teaching the high school class. He was no longer a liturgist. He was no longer asked to visit the shut-ins. Invitations to dinner ceased. In fact, when there was a potluck dinner at the church, they asked him not to go through the line. They brought him his dinner on a paper plate with plastic utensils. He ate alone.

When he became my client, Bill weighed less than 90 pounds. He had sores all over his body and face. He couldn't swallow and could barely talk, which he loved to do. The smell in his room was so bad that I had to rub a mint oil under my nose to endure the smell.

"I have no one. My family stopped coming. Even my pastor doesn't come to visit anymore. I know that I look horrible and they fear that they might get AIDS by being in the same room with me. And the smell in this room from these sores is horrible although I lost my sense of smell a long time ago."

"Dr. Stephenson, how much punishment will God put upon me for the sins I have committed? I fear that even God has abandoned me. Just like my family. Just like my church. Besides you, there is no one that comes. Am I that bad?"

"Bill, people who are ignorant of your disease will act out of fear and ignorance. Are you in pain, Bill?"

"Just the body sores. I can't find any way to find comfort from them. God is really punishing me. I've been a Christian all my life and I know I'm going to die soon. I feel so alone. That even God has abandoned me. It's such a hopeless feeling."

"Bill, is there anything more that I can do for you? I can't change what has happened to you and I want to get angry when I think about it. You don't deserve to come to the end of life all alone."

We stayed together silently for several minutes. I couldn't let this man die without some sense of hope. Then, suddenly, I knew what I had to do. *"Bill, I'll be right back."* I hurried down to the hospital cafeteria and found a roll and hurried back to Bill's room.

"Bill, do you remember when Jesus was coming to the end of his life? Do you remember what he did? You recall that he had a last meal with his disciples. After that dinner, he took a loaf of bread and he broke it and he said, 'Take and eat this and whenever you do it again, remember me. Remember that I never gave up on you. Remember that I will always be with you in life and in death. I will not abandon you. I will be with you always.'"

"Bill, I know you can't eat this, but take this bread and I want you to hold on to it as if your life depended upon it. Hold on to this remnant of remembrance. You are not alone. Christ is with you and you don't have to wait until you die to know that you are with Christ. Not just now, but always."

Bill tried to talk but the tears in his eyes and the look on his face was all that needed to be said. Bill would hold on to that bread for the remaining few days of his life. The nurses tried to open his hand so that they could replace the bread with a fresh one, but he wouldn't let them come near that hand. Bill knew to the very end that he was indeed a child of God.

He had asked me to prepare his body for burial. I took him down to the morgue and on the table laid what was left of Bill. It was a painful and most difficult task. But I washed his body. When it came to his hand, it took every bit of strength for me to pry that hand open and there was but a particle of that bread. The rest had been absorbed into Bill. As I looked at the remaining bread and Bill's body, I realized that I was witnessing the Hope of the world. A Hope that held on to Bill.

A person begins to die
When they cease to
Expect anything from tomorrow.

—*Abraham Miller*

No Name

I was asked to provide counsel to a young married couple who were soon to have a baby. These parents were in their early twenties, poor, and living on the margin of society. Both recovering from a life of major drug addiction.

Their counseling began a few weeks prior to the delivery of their child. The birth of their baby was going to be a major challenge to their recent and fragile freedom from drugs. Why? Their doctor had to tell them that their child would die soon after her birth. She was anencephalic. Her brain was on the outside of her skull and hanging on only by a thread of brain matter to the brain stem.

I would meet with this couple, Jason and Linda, twice a week. Their emotions ran the spectrum. They were frightened, depressed, and angry, but they didn't know what to do with these emotions and they began to take it out on each other. They blamed each other for the "monster" that was soon to come into their lives. Whenever they spoke to each other it was usually in sarcasm and bitterness. "B---h!" "A-----e!" They both felt that someone should be punished for their pain and it came to be toward each other. They had already decided that as soon as the baby was born and died, they would split up and divorce.

The first sessions with them were so painful, so hurtful, so hopeless. It was in the third and final week that I asked, *"What does this baby mean to you?"* For the first time I had caused a shift from them to their child, and they were unable to answer. They looked at each other, hoping that one of them would speak so they could attack them for whatever they would say. However, before I asked the question, I had set some ground rules.

"So far, you have spent all this time tearing each other down. Now it's time to prepare for the birth of your child. What benefit do you find in tearing each other down that will help you cope with not just her birth but also her death? Will her "legacy" be that you will have destroyed your marriage and, quite likely destroy your sobriety? What do you want your daughter to be remembered for?"

"*I don't know,*" said Jason. "*I just want the pain to go away. I want this nightmare to end. I can't get connected to this baby. I don't even want to give her a name.*"

"*She is living because she is inside me,*" said Linda. "*I don't want her to be birthed because then I can no longer prevent her from dying. I know Jason blames me for all this. Perhaps I am, but this baby deserves to be loved and cared for, even if it's for only a few moments. Jason, we both need you, now more than ever.*"

"*I'm sorry, Linda. But I can't take this anymore. I just can't take this anymore.*" Jason stood up and walked to the door. He turned and said, "*Goodbye. I'm sorry, Linda. But you're on your own.*" He left and would never return.

Linda would give birth to her baby by C-section. She would birth her baby without a husband, family, or friends. She asked me to be there and I agreed. I asked her what she planned to do when the baby was born, knowing that her baby would live for only a few minutes.

"*I know that I'm not very much of a Christian, or whatever, but I do believe in God, and I wish I could have her baptized so that I know she would go to heaven. I want to know that she is going to have in death what I could not give her in life.*"

"*Linda, let me see what I can do.*" I reached out to the person on my team who was designated as the spiritual caregiver for our clients. She agreed to assist in a baptism ritual when the baby was born.

It was a dramatic moment. As soon as the baby was born, the doctor placed her on Linda's chest and I put my hands under the baby's head and brain as my colleague baptized her, simply saying, "*I baptize you in the name of God the creator, Son, and Holy Spirit.*" But no name. Linda could not, would not, give her baby a name.

I left the clinic early that morning completely and emotionally drained. The sun was just beginning to rise. As I neared my car, I looked across the street and standing there looking at me was Jason. Our eyes connected for a few moments and then he turned and walked away.

Even to this day, I will wake up early in the morning and be unable to return to sleep, remembering how I took part in the birth and baptism of a baby who died with no name. But I was reminded that God already had given this child a name.

There are times when hope is difficult to find.

Hope is but the dream of those who wake.

—*Matthew Prior*

Faith, Hope, and Love Abide

Kathy was twenty-nine. She was from Santa Barbara, beautiful, rich, entitled, very outgoing, a social animal. She also had an internal spirit that everyone wanted to be around. Her cancer was Hodgkin's Lymphoma. She had tried every treatment, but this cancer was relentless. She came to this well-known cancer treatment center outside of Tijuana to try experimental and non-orthodox treatments.

Patients from all over the world, who had been told to go home and live until they died because there was nothing else that could be done for them, came to this clinic by the hundreds. For two years I did my internship at this facility. Most of my work was in the fifty-bed hospital near the outpatient clinic. I developed an experimental program that was then known as the "death ward."

The death ward consisted of seven beds in the hospital section of the facility for persons too sick to go to the clinic or be moved back home. I also did extensive counseling to other clients at the clinic of the hospital as well as lead a cancer support group three times a week. One of them was at the clinic and this is where I came to know Kathy.

"Kathy, why are you here? I have yet to see you in treatment. Why are you here?"

"I couldn't stand it up in Santa Barbara. Everybody looking at me as if I were already dead. It was claustrophobic. I just had to get out of there, and I had heard about this clinic. I figured, what the hell! I've got nothing to lose. I have no hope of living to celebrate my next birthday. None. I'm down here so that I don't have to hear the goddamn question, 'How are you feeling today?' I am so sick of being seen as sick. Here, I'm just one of the lepers! I am sick and tired of being sick and tired."

"Kathy, would you be interested in spending your day doing something more than just feeling sorry for yourself? We have over 200 patients daily here at the clinic, plus their spouse or parent or whatever. We have another fifty hospital beds up the street. This place doesn't have one volunteer. Anybody working here is paid. I want to offer you the position of Director of Volunteers. I happen to know that you have more money than dirt so your salary will

be free meals and me as your supervisor. And, there will be no charge for the counseling I am going to provide you."

"I don't think I qualify. All my life people served me. I don't remember ever helping anyone."

"If you take the position, I will want you to spend the next two weeks, walking around the two campuses and writing down your observances. What questions seem to be the most common? How are people feeling about being down here? What resources can the clinic provide the people who are down here that would make their stay more meaningful? How can we better communicate with them? What services could we provide these people?"

"What's in it for me?"

"How much time did your doctors say you had?"

"Maybe a year, probably less."

"Take a portion of that and put it into caring for others. People come here and they're frightened and confused and isolated. I want you to be part of reducing that. C'mon, what do you say?"

"I'll give it a try, but can we check in daily?"

"As I am able, Kathy. My plate is pretty full at the hospital."

"Do you know what people are calling you? Dr. Death, because of the death ward you have created? You're lucky that they don't call you Dr. Doom!"

"Geez, I better change that perception. Will you help?"

"Let's get started."

In less than a month, Kathy had two weekly "Make Today Count" programs that had more than fifty people in each one of them. She chaired them and brought in "celebrities" like the Director of the Clinic, the Director of the Hospital, some of the most popular doctors. Every session included testimonials from patients about the care they were receiving. People who were getting ready to go back home and how they felt about being here. She was a woman on a mission. Getting her in for counseling was quite the challenge.

And then the weekly community meal that she hosted (and that was paid for by her). Music and entertainment but again opportunities for patients and their families to share. Every morning, she was at the front door to welcome people coming into the clinic, checking to make sure they were being cared for by this medical facility, physically, emotionally, and spiritually.

But her health was deteriorating and after only three months of volunteering, she was told that she needed to return home while she still could. She agreed and as she was leaving, we had a brief conversation.

"Bill, you have been able to give me a reason to get up each day. I would wake up and sometimes I even forgot that I had cancer. I had purpose and meaning and, this may be a crazy word from someone who is dying, but I had hope. You gave me a chance to express that hope and I will never forget you. In fact, I want to know if you would come and be with me at the very end. I don't want to die with a bunch of "rookies" hanging around. You know what to do and what to say. Will you come?"

"I will sincerely try. Let's see how things go. But before you go, I want you to walk out to the patio area for a moment."

The entire community surprised her with a party of all parties. Staff, patients, even many of the merchants around the facility were there to celebrate the devotion she had given to her project and it would continue on after she left.

Kathy called me nearly every day. When she knew she had less than a month to live she asked me to come to Santa Barbara to be one of her primary support persons. Her brother was her primary and he had his hands full maintaining civility with all of the family and friends that came and went each day at Kathy's huge home up in the hills overlooking Santa Barbara and the ocean.

When I arrived and met Kathy, she came into my arms and just stayed there for the longest of time. I knew that we were both needing that embrace. We talked until her pain became unbearable and forced her to take significant pain medication which managed her pain, but also put her down and out and she hated that.

It was towards the end of the week I arrived that I would come to know why Kathy wanted me there. We both knew we had a strong attraction to each other and how hard it was for me to watch her suffer. One morning, she called me into her room.

"Bill, I can't take this pain any longer. I'm not living, I'm dying and that is something I don't want to prolong. Would you help me to die? I've stashed enough morphine and pain pills, but I can't do it alone. I need you to help me."

She asked me to help her inject enough morphine in her IV drip that would end her life and her suffering. I brought her brother into the room and I explained to him what she wanted me to do. It was illegal but her suffering was immoral. He agreed that assisting her to end her life was the right thing to do.

I sat next to Kathy and together we injected the IV drip with a large dose of morphine and waited for the morphine to take effect.

She said, *"Bill, I'm in love with you, and I know you love me. Thank you for the way you have loved me this past year. Can we kiss goodbye?"*

With tears in our eyes, we kissed for the first and last time. She took a quick breath and collapsed in my arms. The morphine compromised her respiratory system and in minutes she stopped breathing.

It was a good death. But it's one of the few I remember every year. On June 29, I pause to remember Kathy. Her memory gently guided my soul and my way with the many others who would follow.

Hope is an embrace of the unknown.

—*Rebecca Solnit*

CHAPTER THREE

Adults

I have always been fascinated with the way hope becomes realized. Some say it is like giving birth to a newborn. Others see it as a consequence. Still others see it as a gift. I have become convinced that it is developed through relationships. There is some chemical reaction between people who have a relationship that enables hope to be generated into the human soul. That same kind of hope can come with our relationship with God. Hope that is generated into the human soul.

But there is a significant difference between counseling children about hope and counseling adults. Children have little "baggage" as they define hope. They don't bring a history of failed relationships, failed dreams and goals, a list of conditions. It is rare to not find hope in a child. For these reasons, I separated the stories of children from those of the adults so that the hope in a child and the hope in an adult can be seen more clearly.

The testimonies to hope in this chapter about adults speak to the kind of hope that is unique to adults.

Margaret, who found hope in the relationship with her family; and her grace defined those relationships.

Mamie, now completely alone, found hope in an encounter with a stranger.

Two women, Mrs. Elder and Mrs. Collins, both living alone, many miles apart, and having never met, but who found hope through one person they came to trust through the breaking of bread.

Randy, finding hope when he allowed forgiveness to occur.

But that miracle doesn't always work. "A Teachable Moment" describes what I judge to be the most difficult encounter I ever had. No matter how confident I was with terminally ill adults, this case would nearly destroy my career.

It was in my "recovery" from this case that I found the story of Dr. Perl. If she could maintain hope in Auschwitz, then this clinician could move forward as well.

The last two testimonies to adult hope can be found in the hope Jane discovered with her two teenage daughters, who would be orphans. Her legacy to her kids is a remarkable testimony to the powerful relationship she had with her daughters.

And finally, Bill. The punishment he received in relationships with those he cared so much about who betrayed him versus the one who would never abandon him.

Hope. The equation is different and yet the same.

*It is a good place when you have hope
and not expectations.*

—*Danny Boyle*

What Creates Hope?

Where does hope come from? What generates it? How does one sustain it? For those coming to the end of life, what does hope look like? This story, and the five stories following describe the value of gratitude and grace to help find the answers to these questions and discover a unique understanding of hope.

Margaret was seventy-two years old and had been battling cancer for a long time. But she was losing that battle and her time was also running out. That is when she and her family turned to hospice care. For a period of time, I was their counselor and Margaret asked if I would step into her room to meet with her. I offer from my notes the essence of our conversation.

Margaret was sitting up in a wheelchair accompanied by an IV tree carrying her vital pain medication. I could see that she was still in pain, despite the medication, but she also greeted me with a wonderful smile and a cheerful hello.

"I know who you are. You're the hospice counselor. Dr. Stephenson, thank you for coming. I'll get right to the point. I know that my life is soon to end. I am so tired of fighting this disease. I need a break from it and death is going to give me what doctors can't do. I have had some amazing doctors and they have given me more time than I ever expected. And it's been good time. And even when they advised me to stop fighting the cancer, they have stayed with me, giving me their support and advice. I am so grateful for their commitment to an old woman. But now I need someone to teach me how to die and that's hard for me because all I can think about is how much I love to live."

I had heard about Margaret from other staff members and even some of the other patients. They seemed amazed that she had such a hopeful attitude about her losing battle with cancer. She had said to the chaplain, *"Cancer is not my enemy. It's a part of who I am, and I don't house anything in my being that is an enemy. I have made peace with my cancer. I have chosen to not let it be the defining moment of my life."*

She said, *"I have this incredible family. I live alone but I rarely if ever am alone. They have organized this most incredible treatment plan that begins early each day in getting me up and ready for the day. And their attitude is,*

'Treat Margaret as a person who happens to have cancer. Not as a cancer patient.' They have been by my side every moment of this journey. They have given me strength and a reason to live for another day."

"Dr. Stephenson, I have learned hope does not produce gratitude. Quite the contrary. It is gratitude that produces hope. And this is what I want my family to understand. I want them to be filled with gratitude, for the way they all worked together and, despite mistakes here and there, they still remained a family. And therein lies their hope."

"That's what I need from you, Dr. Stephenson. Get them together to talk about this hope that has bonded us together. I know my time is near and they are going to need this hope."

"Margaret, I'm exhausted just listening. But yes, I will bring them together, and yes, your family will come to understand how it is gratitude that brings hope."

By the time I had brought them all together for a conference, Margaret had taken a dramatic turn. She was in and out of consciousness and unable to speak. In the family meeting, Margaret's condition came up. One of her granddaughters, who had given more time to Margaret than anyone in the room, asked, *"Why can't Grandma get well again?"* And a younger grandson, wiser than beyond his years, said, *"Tammy, sometimes our loved ones have to die in order to get well. Grandma will be well soon. She has been the greatest Grandmother ever. And that is where I place my hope."*

Death can be, for some like Margaret, an angel of light. Her "Gratitude Equals Hope" would be her legacy to her family. No, I couldn't teach Margaret how to die but she was able to teach me and her family much about how to live. Gratitude.

A Tibetan saying,
"Tragedy should be utilized as a source of strength."
No matter what sort of difficulties,
how painful the experience is,
If we lose hope, that's our real disaster.

—Dali Lama

How Hope Is Born

I was visiting a client who was in the hospital to undergo an experimental treatment for her advanced form of cancer. We had become good friends and toward the end of our session, we were laughing and having a good time.

Evidently, a patient in the adjoining room had overheard our conversation about how to live until we die, and she asked the nurse if I would come and visit her after I was finished with my client.

I want to pause and paint a picture of the patient I walked in to meet. Day and night, she had to have an oxygen tube in her nostrils in order to stay alive. The cancer was in both lungs and she was slowly suffocating to death. The cancer was also in her bones and joints and back, and she was in constant pain, even though she was heavily medicated. Every movement was agony for her.

This lady would die in this tiny room, alone. Seldom, if ever, did anyone come to visit or offer her a word of comfort. She said, *"They don't know what to say and they can't bear watching me in such pain."*

This woman's mind, however, was as sharp as any mind I knew. This woman's spirit was more lovely than any flower arrangement or any symphony of an orchestra. I sensed I was in the presence of a teacher and my soul was about to be enriched.

I sat down with her and we talked. She said, *"I need to talk to someone who will listen, and I believe you are the one to do that."*

"Yes, ma'am. I will listen, but from time to time, I want to tell you what I hear you saying. Deal?"

"Deal."

For over an hour, this woman would talk about her life, her family, and her faith. She told me what she was proud of and what she was ashamed of. At the end of the hour, we were both exhausted.

As I prepared to leave, I said, *"Mamie, before I go, can I tell you a joke?"*

Her eyes lit up, and I told her a joke. It was very funny. I'm not going to tell you the joke, but it was very funny.

And then she said, *"Dr. Stephenson, can I tell you a joke?"*

She told me one, and, it too was very funny. We both laughed. There was a moment when I felt as if my soul was at one with her soul. There, in that room of death, a seasoned psychotherapist and a cancer-stricken lady, both of us surrounded by the smells of disinfectant and death, giggling like two kids caught with their hands in the cookie jar!

When we finished laughing, we paused and just looked at each other in silence for several moments. I said to Mamie, *"Do you believe in hope?"*

"I do now," she said. *"I had lost it, but I feel it coming back. Thank you."*

"Mamie, I'm leaving this room with more hope than when I came in. From this conversation with you, I just experienced a hope I have been hungering to embrace. Does this make sense?"

"It doesn't have to make sense to me. It needs to make sense to you. But I'm glad I lived long enough to have this conversation. It will carry me into tomorrow and tomorrow may be all I will have. I am grateful. Yes, I believe in hope."

I leaned over and gave her a kiss on her cheek, and then she kissed me. It was a sacred moment. I felt like I wanted to take off my shoes because I knew I was standing on holy ground. We were never to see each other again.

The sky takes on shades of orange
During sunrise and sunset,
The color that gives you hope
That the sun will set
Only to rise again.

—Ram Charan

Do This and Remember

I am convinced that the cruelest form of punishment is having to eat alone. It often befalls those who can no longer participate in their social communities such as church or synagogue.

"What did you do wrong?"

"Arthritis and a broken hip. I'm unable to get out of the house."

"Yeah, that'll do it. And you, what did you do?"

"My husband died and I'm 86."

"Aha! That serves you right!"

Two stories.

I had two women who were both diagnosed as being terminally ill and their physicians asked if I would take their cases to provide them with psychotherapy. Both women were widows and both of them lived alone. These women taught me to understand the power of inclusiveness and hope.

Mrs. Elder. Terminally ill and near the end and living in a skilled nursing facility. I found her room and the staff eventually wheeled her into the room in which I was to conduct the interview.

The first thing I said was, *"What are you in for?"*

She said, *"Talking to myself."*

"Yes, that'll do it."

Apparently, she belonged to a church of over 1000 members with several ministers, choirs, fellowship groups, several women's groups, Bible classes, and groups that took trips.

"How long's it been since anybody from your church came to visit, Mrs. Elder?"

"You're the first person to come visit me in over 3 months and you're not even from the church." Punishment for getting sick and talking to herself. Make her eat alone.

I said, *"Mrs. Elder, may I come and share supper with you once a week? Which night would you prefer?"* She chose Tuesday and every Tuesday for the next four months, I was there at 5:00, waiting for her to arrive.

She said, *"It is so heartening to see someone waiting for me to have a meal rather than me waiting for them. Coming to this meal is something I look forward to every week."*

Hope.

Another client, Mrs. Collins. A woman in her mid-seventies, living in a beautiful home overlooking the Los Angeles basin. She now lived alone since her husband had died. On the mantle were pictures of all her kids and grandchildren who apparently all lived on the East Coast. All of them too busy to come and visit.

She said, *"Sit down and relax. I'll go and fix us some lunch. It won't take long."*

But after a while I got restless sitting there all alone, so I went looking for her. She had a large formal dining room that could seat over a dozen at the table and this table was beautifully adorned with the finest of china and linens with creases two inches deep.

I found Mrs. Collins in the kitchen and I said, *"Mrs. Collins we could have just as easily eaten here in the kitchen."* But she kept at it. Cloth napkins in silver rings. Stemmed crystal ware. Beautiful silverware. Candles in silver candlesticks.

"Mrs. Collins, can't we just eat here in the kitchen?"

"Dr. Stephenson, my doctor told me why you're here, will you please be quiet and sit down."

"Yes, ma'am, I was just going to do that next."

She said, *"Apparently, you don't know what it's like to prepare a meal for one."*

"No ma'am, I don't."

She and I sat at her table together and we had a banquet. All two of us. And she assured me that the number around the table that day was twice as many as she had had in months and months and months.

I would be going to see Mrs. Elder and Mrs. Collins on a regular basis, but always at a time when it was time to eat. It would not be long before their cancers became so overwhelming that they could not host or eat with me. But the stories. They kept repeating the times we sat together and ate together. That was the best "therapy" I could have offered. It was amazing to see the hope come into their lives, even if it were for just a few minutes. And the stories. Oh, the stories they would tell of times they had meals with their families, with their friends, and those special times with their husbands. Not to mention the many times they would recall when we had a meal together and the stories we shared. Hope indeed.

When you're at the end of your rope,
Tie a knot and hold on.

—*Theodore Roosevelt*

Father's Day

Randy Johnson was brought into the hospice one day before his 68th birthday. When Randy was admitted, he was angry and hostile, abrupt and extremely restless. When he was asleep, he would moan, as if something terribly wrong had happened.

When asked if everything was okay, he wouldn't answer. The staff knew that he had some unfinished business that he had to deal with if he was to have a "good death." His physical signs were rapidly deteriorating, but he wouldn't die. He wouldn't let go. It was as if something deep within him would not permit death.

I talked to his son to see if he knew what it was. From the expression on his face, I knew that a family secret was about to be revealed. He said, *"I'm not his only child. He has a daughter in Boston. My dad disowned her nine years ago because she married someone of another race. From his point of view, she had committed the unpardonable sin. He said he would never forgive her."*

I went in to see Randy again. It was time to have a serious conversation.

"Randy, I understand that you and your daughter are estranged. I sense that this may be what is called, 'unfinished business.' If you are able, can you talk to me about your relationship with your daughter?"

Silence filled the room for several minutes. Randy finally realized that I wasn't going to leave and he began to share with me what had happened.

"Nine years ago, my daughter surprised me by announcing her engagement to a man I had never met. She explained to me that the reason I never met him was that he was Black, and she feared that I would respond negatively. Which I did, but only out of my concern for her and what I judged to be a life-long battle with racism. I asked when they had planned to get married and she told me that they were going to have a civil ceremony when they got back to Boston and that I was not being invited to attend."

"Dr. Stephenson, I was hurt and angrily shouted back, 'Then don't buy a round trip ticket because you and your boyfriend are not welcomed in this house.' And I turned and walked away. We haven't seen or spoken to each

other since. Yes, I guess I do have unfinished business and there's nothing I can do about it." He then rolled away from me. He was done with this conversation.

I needed to make a phone call to Boston. *"Jessica, I'm Dr. Stephenson and I'm your father's therapist and I understand that your brother has kept you current with your father's condition."*

"Yes," she said, *"He spoke to me last night and indicated that my father has maybe a day or two left. I have wanted to come, but I feared that my presence would only give him more pain and anguish. I love my father and it pains me that he will die not knowing this."*

"Jessica, after a serious conversation with your father, I urge you, for his sake as well as yours, to get on the first plane to Seattle and I can assure you that it will be worthwhile. You will not bring him more pain and anguish. In fact, quite the opposite. But I need an immediate response so that I can encourage your father to fight for another day."

"I just finished booking a flight and I arrive at noon."

"Good, Jessica, you're doing the right thing."

I went back to speak to Randy. *"Randy, I need another day from you, and I need you to be conscious. Can you do that?"*

"I think so, but why?"

She arrived with her brother and waited patiently as the staff went in and prepared Randy for visitors. I escorted them to his room. She stood in the doorway of his room. There was this deafening silence. They just stared at each other.

Then, with all the strength he had left in his life, he opened his arms and she ran to receive them and he said the words that would free him forever. The words that would bring hope and healing to him and her: *"Jessica, I'm so sorry. Please, forgive me."*

She brushed away his tears as well as her own. She sat on his bed and neither said anything for the longest time and then she said to him, cupping his face in her hands, *"Daddy, all is forgiven. Please, Daddy, let it go because I have."*

There were many more tears. They held one another and talked about old times. He learned that he was now a grandfather and there were pictures to see and there was much laughter.

That night, his vital signs were stable and strong. But then an amazing thing began to happen. Around 11:30, he said he was very tired, and he just needed to rest, but he didn't want his children to leave. I quickly wrote them a note: *"Don't leave. He's letting go. Hold on to each other and tell him you love him."*

Jessica and Hank each held one of Randy's hands as his breathing became shallow and his eyes closed for the last time.

But the bitterness was gone from his face. All of his unfinished business had been put to rest. It was a good death. I looked at my watch and a new day had begun. It was Sunday. It was also Father's Day. Forgiveness and hope found each other.

Start every day with a new hope.
Leave bad memories behind.
And have faith for a better tomorrow.

—*Unknown*

A Teachable Moment

Monica was just twenty-seven. She was single. She called herself a born-again Christian. She had no family that came to visit her, as I recall. She was dying of cancer. She asked for me.

I would come to her bedside, and we would talk. Well, she did the talking. She talked incessantly. She talked about her childhood and adolescence. She talked about both of her marriages. She talked about her two miscarriages and one abortion. She owned a lot of unresolved grief and a load of guilt that clashed with her beliefs.

But throughout all her conversations she kept reminding me, or herself, how she had come to know Jesus and the conversional moment when she accepted Christ into her life. It was just after she had been diagnosed with fourth stage lymphocytic leukemia.

She shared with me the extensive and painful treatment she had undergone. She said, *"My fellow church members had been so supportive in the beginning, but now that I have been diagnosed as terminal, they seem less so."* She said, *"They don't know what to say so they stay away."*

She was not the same Monica they had known. She now had no hair, she was emaciated and in constant need of transfusions. There would be no remission for her. She said when people looked at her she could see their fear. Her visitor's registration book was nearly empty.

She seemed dismayed, unsure, anxious. I continued to counsel her on her current state, and I remained committed to assisting her in staying in the moment; staying in the present; knowing her death was imminent.

She continued each session with her confidence in Jesus and that he would save her so she could go on missionary trips around the world. She said, *"I am determined that when I get out of the hospital, I will dedicate the rest of my life to service for others."*

She continued to be in terrible pain, but she refused all pain medications. The pain medications could manage the pain without rendering her unconscious, but she felt the need to stay alert and wait for one more round of chemotherapy that would save her life. But there would not be one more round.

Late one weekend afternoon, when many of the patients in the hospice were out visiting family or going for a walk, Monica used that time to talk to the staff about her faith and how she was ready as she said, "to go be with Jesus." Her ability to thrive was declining rapidly and early that same evening, she collapsed.

She was put in her bed and the hospice team did everything they could to make her comfortable. She was close to death, but she asked that I come to her bedside as soon as possible. When I arrived, she began to cry. It was a frightened cry, like a small child who was lost and there was no one to help her.

"Dr. Stephenson, is it time for me to die? I'm not ready yet. I'm not ready yet. I don't want to die. I don't want to die! Please. Hold me. I'm so scared!"

I reached down and took her in my arms and held her, but she continued to cry, and her distress now became known by everyone around us. It was as if no one could understand what needed to be done. Monica suddenly hemorrhaged. She began to expel blood from her mouth, nose, and rectum.

She was well aware of her fading consciousness and died soon after.

I don't remember much of what transpired after that. Nurses said I was covered in blood. They tried to speak to me, but they could tell I was not able to hear them. They say I was unable to speak or respond to any voice for nearly three days. Weeks went by and I had night terrors that disrupted both my personal and professional life. Sleep meant nightmares. I wasn't fit to see clients. I lost weight.

Therapy, especially group therapy, helped me get past what I judged to be my biggest failure. I would have other "failures" who would challenge my commitment to this work I had chosen for myself, but Monica's death was my "teachable moment." I learned that I had to take each assignment separately and avoid "glopping" them all into my "caseload." In therapy, I set my ego aside so that my heart could have a larger role. My capacity to counsel clients who were terminally ill, no matter what their age, was not going to be my epitaph or on my gravestone. I also learned that I needed someone or a way of working through my grief that I kept denying.

All this was learned from this death and more. My hope descended into despair but through counseling, I found a new understanding of a hope that will never abandon me and a hope I could model for others. It was a teachable moment.

Neither should a ship rely on one small anchor,
Nor should a life rest on a single hope.

—*Epictetus*

Tomorrow…

Those I have worked with who were facing a terminal illness would often comment about the need to stay in the present. To make today count. Hope is not found in focusing on the future but living in the present. Each day, despite the diagnosis or the prognosis, we choose to live in the present, but at the same time, to keep choosing to have a future. Even if that future is six months or less.

I share this story not because it is morbid, but because it is miraculous. If hope could ever be found in Auschwitz, then surely it can be found in the conflict of a nation wracked with racism and divisiveness. It's about an eighty-two-year-old Jewish physician, Gisella Perl. She tells of her experience in the concentration camp. She said:

"The greatest crime at Auschwitz was to be pregnant. The so-called 'doctor of death,' Josef Mengele, performed savage medical experiments on prisoners and particularly on women, the physically handicapped, and twins. He was in charge of deciding who would go to the showers of death."

"Dr. Mengele told me that it was my duty to report every pregnant woman to him. He said they would go to another camp for better nutrition, even for milk."

Women began to run directly to him, telling him, 'I'm pregnant.' I learned that they were all taken to the search block to be used as guinea pigs and then two lives would be thrown into the crematorium. I decided that never again would there be a pregnant woman in Auschwitz."

And then, Dr. Perl tells how she interrupted the pregnancies in the night on a dirty floor using only, she said…

"…my dirty hands. If I had not done it, both mother and child would have been cruelly tortured and murdered." She said, *"I had no bed, no bandages, no drugs, no instruments. I saw every disease brought about by torture, starvation, filth, lice, and rats."*

"But," she said, *"I had one thing that I could give these women. The one thing I had was the spoken word."*

She said, *"I treated patients with my voice, telling them beautiful stories. Telling them that one day we would have birthdays again. One day, we would sing again. I didn't know when it was Rosh Hoshana, but I had a sense of it when the weather cooled. So, I made a party with the bread, lard, and dirty pieces of sausage we received for meals."*

And she said, *"Tonight will be the New Year. Tomorrow, a better year will come."* [4]

If those women could have a party in a death camp, then when we or someone we love is experiencing all kinds of crisis and stress, disappointment and disillusionment....Even in the midst of all that, we can still be a family, a friend, a lover. We can hope in God. To say to one another enough times until we believe it: *"Tomorrow, a better year will come."* That is the one thing we can all do. To be the spoken word. To say again and again to those we love and care for who are going through a difficult time: *"Tomorrow, a better year will come."*

It is of hope that you suffer.
It is through hope that you'll change things.

—*Maxine Legace*

When All Hope Seems Gone

Every once in a while, I will have that experience where I know I had just visited the Kingdom of God. Several years ago, I was facilitating a small group of men and women who were all dying of AIDS. Twice a week, they would meet to share their "story" of living with this horrible disease. They often called themselves lepers because they only had fellow lepers to relate to. Everyone else had excluded them.

One early, very rainy evening, as we sat in a circle together, there was a silence in the room. The only sound was the pounding of the rain against the windows. We didn't even have the lights on. The atmosphere clearly represented the spirit of hopelessness and alienation that many in the group were feeling.

Then, the eldest person in the group, a Jewish man in his late seventies, said, *"I brought with me to the group this bread that was just made by a family member. It's still warm and it tastes so good. I want to share it with all of you."*

We passed the bread around the circle, each taking a healthy slice and putting soft butter that he had also brought on our slices. We all waited until everyone had a slice of bread. He blessed the bread and we began to eat as the rain continued to pound against the windows.

Moments later, we realized the rain had stopped. We looked out and the clouds were breaking up and the most beautiful sunset replaced the storm and a rainbow began to take shape. We stood up and put our arms around each other and shoulder to shoulder we looked out the window as the sun began to set and the rainbow poured into our meeting room. In that moment, the bread we shared, the storm, and then the rainbow, the unconditional trust we had between each other, all this instilled in each of us a special kind of hope. A divine hope. An eternal hope.

They all died within weeks of each other but in that circle, we each got a taste of the eternal kingdom. We each felt surrounded by a great cloud of witnesses, reassuring us that the Kingdom of God was not far.

*Learn from yesterday, live for today, hope for tomorrow.
The important thing is not to stop questioning.*

—*Albert Einstein*

CHAPTER FOUR

Hope in Other Circumstances

The stories in this chapter are not about persons who were terminally ill or had a loved one who was terminally ill. This chapter illustrates how fragile hope can be when we are facing a crisis or are vulnerable to being lost.

Complicated grief is often the "bullet" that can destroy a person's hope. This was true in the first story of Mrs. Truxton.

Ms. Thompson, who like Margaret in the previous chapter, discovered that gratitude generates hope but not the other way around.

Stephen, who had everything and then....

Marion had her hope restored and chose to not let a disease take it away.

Two suicide attempts. Both believing that there was no other way to escape their pain.

Finally, Laurie, who chose to "stuff" her hurt with her mother for more than twenty years but finally claimed the courage that would free them both.

A little belief, a little faith, a little hope
Is sometimes all that is needed to see the light.

—*Swati Singh*

And So It Goes

It was late and the storm was relentless, even for the Pacific Northwest. As I turned in to go to bed, I was thinking of how relieved I felt that I didn't have to be anywhere that night. Just as I crawled into bed, I heard someone pounding over and over again on my front door and the person seem to be calling out my name. I was alone in my Seattle home and all the lights were out.

I got up, put on my bathrobe, and went to the door. I turned on the porch light and yelled through the front door, *"Who is it? Who's out there?"*

A moaning, sobbing voice responded as the person continued pounding on the door. *"Please, please let me in. I can't live like this any longer! Please!"*

I opened the door and in fell an elderly woman, soaked from the rain, her hair was disheveled and dripping from the storm. She was shivering from the cold, wet, sobbing through it all, and unable to make any sense of her situation. She introduced herself as Marion Truxton.

I turned on the heat and lights, lit a fire, and started the coffee. I sensed that this was going to be a long night. I suggested she go in and shower and change into some dry clothes I had selected I thought she could wear.

I said, *"Mrs. Truxton, I insist that you do these few things, or I won't be able to help you. But if you shower and change, this will give you a few moments to breathe and calm yourself so that we can talk this through. Otherwise, I need to call 911."*

Thirty minutes later, she came back into the living room, sat down, and just stared at the floor. There was little improvement in her state of mind. *"Why did you come here, Mrs. Truxton, and how did you find me?"*

She said, *"I heard you give a lecture about your work with the terminally ill and with those in significant grief. And, you're in the phone book. Dr. Stephenson. I need your help. Ever since my husband died, I haven't been able to function. I can't live like this any longer. You've got to take my case. You've got to!"*

I never see clients in my home and rarely see adults without children in a life-threatening crisis, but saying no to someone in distress at midnight didn't seem like a good idea. *"Mrs. Truxton, tell me your story."*

"Just before my husband died, we had a terrible argument. Before we went to bed, I screamed at him, 'I wish you were dead!' The next morning, I woke up, and next to me was my dead husband."

She said, *"I am responsible for my husband's death. It's my fault. I have been burdened by this guilt. I was too distraught to go to the funeral. I often don't get out of bed. I don't know how to live alone. I cry constantly. I rarely venture out of the house. I've stopped seeing my friends or going to my church because I just keep crying. Even my children have grown weary of me and they don't want the grandchildren around me. My world has come to an end and all I want to do is die."*

As the hour of counseling came to a close, I decided to extend it to two. Both of us exhausted, we set up a schedule of times we would meet, including the next day. I asked her if she thought she could drive home and she reassured me that she was very capable. The storm outside and the storm inside seemed to be abating.

"Mrs. Truxton, do you have feelings of wanting to kill yourself?"

"Not anymore, Dr. Stephenson. I feel like I have some hope that I haven't had for a long time."

"What does hope look like for you?"

"I have felt such shame. People who hear my story look at me with that 'How could you?' look. As if I should be ashamed of myself. I feel judged and at least partially at fault for his death. One woman said to me, 'Someday, you will have to account for your words.' But I don't see that in your eyes. I feel safe with you and I haven't felt that for a long time. That's where I find hope."

Just as she was leaving, I asked her, *"By the way, Mrs. Truxton, I meant to ask you, how long ago did your husband die?"*

She said, *"It's been eleven years ago yesterday. And it seems like it was only yesterday."*

It would take several months of therapy and medication management to resolve the issues in her life. But grief is a strange animal and time doesn't heal all wounds. In fact, for Mrs. Truxton, her watch had stopped.

Hope is a waking dream.

—*Aristotle*

The Gift of Thanksgiving and Hope

I knew her only as Ms. Thompson. She had her spot where she panhandled for change, just outside an old abandoned church on a street corner in downtown Seattle near my office. I passed her every day and each day for several months I would make a small donation to her support. We became more and more acquainted with each other as time passed. She always wore the same tattered overcoat whether it was winter or summer.

Then Ms. Thompson disappeared. She was no longer at her station of contact. Others who also knew her wondered what had happened to her. We asked around but no one could explain her disappearance. Time passed and we all moved on with our lives.

Then one day, there she was at her old station on the corner in front of the abandoned church. But this time without a sign asking for help. I went over to her to give her a donation and she stopped me and said, *"Not today. I no longer need your donation. I now have a job and I'm doing okay. I'm here because I want to thank those of you who gave me their regular support when I was in great need. I am here to return thanks. Please, take this gift of my thanksgiving."*

In her small wrapped gift was a doughnut. She was handing these to all of us who had given her support in the past year. A gift-wrapped doughnut. She was indeed a woman filled with thanksgiving and hope.

Hope is a state of mind, not of the world.
Hope, in this deep and powerful sense,
Is not the same as joy that things are going well,
or willingness to
Invest in enterprises that are obviously
heading for success,
But rather an ability to work for something
because it is good.

—Valav Havel

A Hope Redefined

I had been asked to prepare a community in Colorado for the death of a person that was revered by all. It was a small town and the grief would be experienced by all of its civic leaders. I would spend two weeks conducting several small groups focusing on loss and how they would cope with the death of someone they all loved and respected. It was a monster of an assignment and it would conclude with a community meeting in the high school auditorium.

The morning after I had arrived, I was sitting in the local coffee shop having breakfast, and in came a gentleman in a wheelchair. He was quadriplegic and was accompanied by a gentleman who was obviously his primary caregiver and chauffeur. His van outside was huge.

When their breakfast came his manservant would cut up his food and place it on a special mechanically powered fork that he would use to eat. He saw me watching him, smiled, and asked if I would care to join them.

He said, *"I know who you are and why you are here and those of us who live here hope your time with us will be as rewarding as we hope ours will be. This town has had some major losses in the last few years and I expect even more in the near future. We hope you can teach us how to grieve as a community as well as individually. I know that's a tall order, but we could really use your expertise. What we want to know is how we can better care for each other in the days ahead."*

I would learn that this encounter was planned. He had intentionally come to the restaurant to meet me. His name was Stephen and we spent the next three hours in that restaurant, getting to know each other and telling stories that would describe our lives.

I never knew a man who was more radiant, more relevant, more energizing than Stephen. He had such passion for his community and hope. Hope was his strength and I could tell that to be around him very long, one would acquire that attitude. We would spend the next two days talking about our lives, our careers, and his community. I would learn how he was able to have such hope despite his handicap.

Stephen was a very successful businessman in the exploration of natural gas. Thirteen years before our encounter, when he was forty years old, he was anxiously waiting for news of a major natural gas discovery to occur. He said, *"I had so much nervous energy and no patience waiting out the time. I noticed that storm clouds would bring a major storm and I decided to climb up on the roof to clean the rain gutters. As I was backing up to get off the roof I forgot about how a few years earlier I had cut out a portion of the overhang to allow a pine tree to continue its growth and I fell through that cut-out and my life would change forever."*

In a matter of seconds, he would go from being a long-distance runner and avid skier to a quadriplegic. I asked him: *"How do you go from running marathons and looking for places to dig for natural gas to being confined to a wheelchair?"*

"Bill, I had it all, but I really had nothing. My life was all about me. How much money could I make? How many competitions could I enter in skiing, running, fishing to name just a few? I had no patience for anyone who got in my way of winning. And then it all changed. I was in massive depression and wishing I could find a way to end my life. My only hope was to find a way that would bring the least amount of pain to my family. And there was none."

"But as time passed, I learned that three things had to happen. The first thing I had to do was adjust. The second thing I had to do was adjust. And the third thing I did was adjust. I went from living a me-centered lifestyle and being an athlete to being a spiritual athlete and community leader."

"Hope was found when my oldest daughter sat down with me and looked me square in the eyes and said, 'Dad, you have always been an inspiration to me. Ever since I was a little girl, I looked to you for answers, solutions, forks in the road I was facing. You are my hero and you are a hero to so many others as well. Dad, you've got to know how much we look to you for hope. Whenever I get down, I think about you and what it must be like to get through your day. I can't imagine. Yet you do it with such grace. Don't give up hope, Dad. Just find a way to redefine it. You've got so much to contribute, and I want to be a part of it.'"

I would learn that he was the one who had retained my services and he would eventually join me at the community meeting and together we would talk about looking outward and how to care for others.

He said, "*I had to redefine who I was. I had to find a new purpose for my life. I decided to find meaning for my life in the way I would treat and support others less fortunate. I am a very wealthy man, and before I die, I want to have my wealth used to give life to others. I am having a wonderful time watching how lives are being changed and all because of my fall off of a roof. I have become an ambassador for hope.*"

Needless to say, I know that my contribution to that community was helpful and I have remained in communication with many of its town leaders. But when I remember being on the stage in the school at the end of my stay, all I can remember was the message Stephen gave to his fellow citizens and to this very humbled therapist.

*Hope is the patient and trustful willingness
to live without closure,
Without resolution, and still be content and even happy
Because our Satisfaction is now at another level and our
Source is beyond ourselves.*

—Richard Rohr

A Bitter Pill To Swallow

"She's a damn slut is what she is!" exclaimed Jack to his wife, sitting next to him.

"This is what I was trying to tell you over the phone, Dr. Stephenson. He is constantly yelling and berating me. For no reason, he becomes very agitated and explodes. Dr. Stephenson, we have been married for over forty-five years, but since the death of our granddaughter he has become a monster."

"Screw you!" exclaimed Jack to Marion.

Jack and Marion came to me for counseling. They knew me because I had worked with their teenage granddaughter who died of a cancerous brain tumor. I had agreed to see them for counseling because I was willing to see any family members for grief counseling. But this one was special.

"Jack, please! Stop it. You have no idea how deep that hurts. I lost a granddaughter too and you don't see me trying to take it out on you. Dr. Stephenson, life is too short, and I am not going to take this any longer. I'm leaving him."

There was then just silence in the room. I asked Marion if I could speak with Jack alone and she abruptly got up and left the room, but not without Jack murmuring, *"B----."*

When she was out of the office, I remained silent, as did Jack for several minutes as he stared down at the floor, mumbling.

"Jack, what's going on? Why are you so angry?"

"Me? I'm not angry. I'm as happy as a lark, which is why I'm wondering what I'm doing here. Yes, I miss Julie, my granddaughter, but other than that, I'm doing just fine."

"Not according to Marion," I said.

"Marion. Who the hell is Marion?"

I stared at him for several minutes as he looked around the room, the ceiling, the floor, his watch, but never at me. I got up and asked Jack to walk with me. I escorted him to the door and asked him to sit in the lobby. I asked an associate to keep an eye on him and then said, *"Marion, would you come into my office for a few minutes?"* and she did. I sat next to her in the chair vacated by Jack. I calmly said, *"Marion,"* and she burst into tears and wept for several minutes.

"Marion, before we do any more counseling sessions, I must insist that Jack, and perhaps you as well, need to make an appointment with your primary doctor and get a thorough check-up. After that, then we can proceed. Will you agree?"

"Yes. I will call as soon as I get home."

"Better still," I said, *"I want you to call right now while you have the privacy to do so."*

She called and made an appointment. I asked if she would give me permission to speak with her doctor and she agreed. I explained to him my relationship to Jack and Marion and voiced my concern without alarming Marion.

We scheduled our next appointment for a week later, after their meeting with their primary doctor. Marion came alone.

"I thought it was hopeless. His abuse was intolerable. He wanders around the house swearing and talking to himself."

"But Marion, you don't seem so tense today as you were last week. Why not?"

She said, *"After our examinations, our doctor called me into his office and that is when I heard the word that changed everything: Alzheimer's."*

"Marion, I feared that it might be something like that after I spoke with Jack alone."

"The doctor doesn't think he will live for more than a year. He said that Jack will need special care in less than six months. I'm losing him but now I understand what has happened to him. He must be so confused, and you can see how frightened he is. Today, I asked him if he would tell me his name and he just stared at me. I knew he couldn't tell me."

"But what about you, Marion? Last week you were at your wit's end."

"But now I understand, Dr. Stephenson. My hope is in the forty-five years we had that were wonderful years. I won't let this last year we have together

be our defining moment. And I'm not alone. Our family now know, and we have made a commitment to give Jack all the love we can give, and they have assured me that I won't have to do this alone."

"Dr. Stephenson, I know you only work with kids, but I need your help."

"Marion, I will be there for you and not just until Jack dies, but I will be there for you as you struggle with his death and learning to live without him there."

"I had lost all hope. Now I have a reason to get out of bed each day. I am going to live my vows I gave to Jack forty-five years ago. I'm going to love him whether he knows it or not."

It was a rocky time, the next few months. But then Jack stopped being so abusive and he became more like a child and was grateful for everything that was being done for him. His death was peaceful, and his entire family was there as they watched Marion sitting on his bed beside him, holding his head in her arms and singing to him.

Hope comes in so many flavors.

Hope is a thing with feathers,
That perches in the soul,
And sings the tune without the words
And never stops at all.

—Emily Dickinson

Balancing on One Foot

I fish on a pier in San Diego that extends over the ocean for several hundreds of feet. A wide variety of people walk that pier each day, many of them tourists. The walk is long and at the end of the pier is a beautiful view of surfers, rolling waves, and the pier itself. There's also a restaurant in the middle that makes fantastic breakfast burritos.

As a counseling therapist, I am aware that on too many occasions this is also a place where some come to solve their pain by jumping off the end of the pier. I have prevented four suicide attempts while fishing on this pier. This is the story of Jacqueline.

It was a foggy morning, but the sun would break through within the hour. I was fishing at the very end of the pier. There were only a few of us there because it's much colder at the end of the pier and a longer walk to the bathroom.

As I was throwing my line over the rail and into the water, I noticed three tourists walking toward me. It appeared to be a mother, father, and their teenage daughter. I could hear some of their conversation and the mother and father suggested breakfast at the café that was just opening. They agreed but their daughter asked to wait a little longer. She would meet them shortly in the café. The parents began the walk and their daughter began to walk toward the end of the south "T" of the pier. I went back to fishing.

However, I sensed that something wasn't right. In the suicide attempts I have stopped on this pier I knew each time that something wasn't right before they attempted to jump. This young lady was no exception. I turned back to my pole and began to reel it in for no reason. When I had finished reeling in my line, I turned to find this young girl had climbed up on one of the tall poles and was precariously balancing on one foot as she looked down at the broiling water below.

I carefully walked toward her perch on the pole and began a conversation with her. *"Good morning. My name is Bill and I'm a counselor. Would you tell me yours?"*

"Yes, my name is Jacqueline."

"How old are you, Jacqueline? And, do you go by Jackie?"

"I'm fifteen and how did you know? Yes, I go by Jackie."

"Jackie, tell me you are balancing yourself on that pole because you are practicing for the Olympics in the balance beam."

"No, but I am a gymnast."

"That explains how you got up there so quickly. How long do you plan on maintaining that position before you climb down, because if you are planning on killing yourself, I have to tell you that you will fail. You will fail because if you jump into that water, then I'm going to have to jump in as well and stop you from killing yourself. So, be mindful that if you jump you are putting my life in danger and I don't want to die."

"Jackie, are you pregnant?"

"How did you know? I've been trying to tell my parents but I'm afraid they will kill me! Bill, I'm at the end of my rope."

Suddenly, we heard a scream coming from near the café and we could both see her parents running toward us.

"Jackie, are you prepared to jump knowing that they will have witnessed your suicide?"

"I hadn't planned it this way. Oh, I don't know what to do."

"Jackie, you have a tough conversation in front of you, but let me join you, and then you won't feel so alone with this."

"Jackie, this isn't the first time you've attempted suicide, is it?"

She gave a big sigh and said, *"No, I tried to kill myself when my boyfriend dumped me. I'm just so tired of disappointing everybody. I want to stop the pain."*

I extended my hand to her and said, *"Before your parents get here, take my hand and I'll help you down. Then let's go sit down and the four of us will get things straightened out."*

There was a long pause as we looked at each other and then slowly her hand reached out. I took it and helped her down and to safety. Her parents began to arrive, and I quickly walked toward them. I introduced myself and asked them to come toward their daughter with calm and compassion. She didn't need hysterical parents at this time. I asked them to pause and take a breath and then go to her.

Not far behind the parents were the police. From previous suicidal attempts, they knew who I was, and they became less concerned. But they had a job to do and had to interview everyone for their required report. I facilitated their interrogation, as well as Jackie's revealing of her secrets and before we realized it, it was lunchtime.

I bought them lunch and we continued talking about Jackie's painful predicament. I asked Jackie to sign a "safe contract" and she promised to carry it on her person at all times. Her parents agreed to cut their vacation short and get Jackie into counseling and also a peer support mental health program.

"Jackie, here is my card. If you need someone to listen through what you are struggling with, just give me a call. Jackie, before I leave, can you tell me how you feel?"

"Dr. Bill, I had no hope of getting past this. Now, I know I can. No, change that. As you said to me, I will get past this. I will not disappoint you. I will stay safe."

"Jackie, stay safe for your sake. I'm going to stay in touch and thank you for agreeing to give me updates. And one last thing: Good luck in trying out for the Olympics. You proved today that you might have a shot. Let that hope you have now flow into that goal as well."

One postscript. Jackie didn't make it into the Olympics, but she gave birth to a beautiful baby girl and continues to live with her parents and she has so much hope that her daughter reinforces every day. Suicide is no longer a part of her daily life. When they come again for vacation, she has agreed to let me teach her how to fish.

We must accept finite disappointment but never lose infinite hope.

—*Martin Luther King, Jr.*

Listening To My Heart

I fish. There's something about fishing that gives me calm and connection. I fish on a pier in San Diego that spans more than six hundred feet out over the Pacific Ocean. On any given day, there will be more than thirty others who will be throwing their line over the side. We get to know each other, those of us who are "regulars." But mixed into our lot will be some people who are homeless, and the resident walkers and also many tourists will take the long walk out to the end of the pier.

In the middle of the pier is a café with fantastic breakfast burritos. I fish here because I also get to observe people, all coming with different agendas. It's also a place where some will come and walk to the end but not come back. The riptide is so severe at the end of the pier that if you jump off from there you won't come back to the surface. This is the story of one of them. Her name was Amy.

Early one morning, I was standing at the entrance to the pier, talking with some fellow fishermen and we were all about to walk out further along the pier to our favorite places to fish. But I noticed a well-dressed young lady about to go on the pier. Too well dressed for such an occasion as not to be noticed.

As she was about to pass me, I said, *"Good morning. How's it going for you today?"*

She stopped and looked at me for what seemed a very long moment and then she said some*thing with* no emotion at all: *"I'm going to walk to the end of the pier, but I'm not coming back."*

I immediately knew that my fishing for that day was not going to happen. I walked closer to her so that I could talk to her in a calm voice. *"As you are walking on the pier, may I walk with you? There's a café in the middle of the pier and they make great coffee. Can I buy you a cup? And as we walk, would you tell me about yourself? My name is Bill and I'm a counseling psychologist. I sense that you are in a lot of hurt right now and I want you to tell me about it."*

"My name is Amy and I'm from Phoenix. I came up here because I was promised a job and some girls I had known in college said that I could live with them and share the apartment. But when I got here there was no job and these girls had given the space in the apartment to someone else and then someone broke into my car and stole all my stuff, including my phone and computer. I am so devastated that all I want to do is die and that's why I'm here and that's what I'm going to go and do!"

We continued to walk together in silence and as we neared the café I said to Amy, *"Your day is worse than you thought. Not only did you not get the job, or have a place to live, but you're also not going to jump off this pier. Today you will not kill yourself."*

She remained unresponsive. I got her a cup of coffee and we continued our walk to the end of the pier as the sun began to peek over the horizon. We stopped to look at the sun rise, overlooking the eastern rails of the pier. In the water were dozens of surfers and on the pier were the many fishermen throwing their lines into the sea.

"Amy, do you see all these people in and around this pier? This is their pier. It's a very important part of their life. How do you think they will feel if you tried to kill yourself from their pier?"

"I don't think they would care. They don't know me. Why should they care?"

"They may not know you personally. But to watch another human being suddenly die is going to have a major emotional effect on them. Many will wish they hadn't been here today. Some may not want to come back. Others will grieve because they witnessed your death. No, Amy, your death will have quite an impact upon them. Not to mention your family and friends. Can you imagine how they will feel? How do I tell your parents?"

With tears in her eyes, she spoke trying to catch her breath at the same time, *"I just don't know what to do, where to go, who to turn to! I feel so alone!"*

"Amy, I want you to do something for me. Actually, I want you to do something for yourself. Right now, you're thinking and making decisions from out of your head. Take a moment and just breathe. And then, I want you to

ask yourself, 'What does my heart say about all this? What is my heart saying to me right now?'"

She took a moment and then she fell into my arms and just sobbed. Several minutes later I escorted her to the café to use the bathroom and sit and continue our conversation.

"I'm not going to hurt myself any longer, Dr. Stephenson."

"Amy, I prepared for you what I call a safe contract. If you begin to feel suicidal, I want you to look at this and remember you telling me that you were safe and wouldn't self-harm. And here is a list of places to help you get home. Here is my phone and I want you to call someone back home to tell them you are on your way back."

She did as I asked and then signed the "safe contract." I walked her to the entranceway to the pier, gave her a hug, and wished her well. She also had my card and knew she could call anytime.

As she neared her car, she turned to me, placed her hand over her heart, and mouthed so I could understand, *"I'm listening to my heart."* She turned, got in her car, and drove away.

Amy had come to believe that "ending it all" would be doing everyone else a favor and, she would no longer have to face the grim struggle of beginning again. But she was able to let go of all the failures she had recently endured and, with just a readjustment of her "framework" she was able to choose to create a new beginning.

The best way to not feel hopeless
is to get up and do something.
Don't wait for good things to happen to you.
If you go out and make some good things happen,
you will fill the world with hope,
you will fill yourself with hope.

—*Barack Obama*

Mother's Day

Laurie was thirty-seven and the mother of a beautiful four-year-old daughter. She was the wife of a colleague and I agreed to be her counselor despite the fact that I was stepping outside of my area of expertise which was counseling persons with a life-threatening illness. She said, *"My problem is with my mother. For years we have had a polite and civil relationship but now that I have a daughter of my own, I want to have a deeper and more genuine relationship with her."*

"How long has this been going on?" I asked.

"Since I went away to college, I think. Maybe longer. My mom has never been very demonstrable with her love. In fact, I don't ever remember her saying. 'I love you' to me. And now she wants me to come for Mother's Day, which I haven't shared with her as far back as I can remember. We send cards and exchange text messages but not face-to-face."

"I sense that you want to change your relationship. Do you think she wants to be closer to you?"

"Since I became the mother of my daughter, I just can't let this go. I don't want this to go on any longer. It's been twenty years and I want to go there and find a way to love my mom. Every time we go back and visit there's a sense of aloofness and distance between us. I want that to stop. I don't want my daughter to grow up with a grandmother that she can't be close to."

"I want you to come back in two days, but in that time, I want you to write down what childhood memories keep coming in the way of your relationship. Bring your notes back and together let's rehearse what you want to say but in a thoughtful way so that she can hear your concerns and not turn you away."

She went back to her childhood home just a few weeks after our conversation. It was Mother's Day and she had not celebrated this with her mother face-to-face since she was a senior in High school. She was in the kitchen with her mother, helping to prepare the family dinner. As she was working with her hands, her head bowed, she began this long-awaited conversation with her mother. A conversation she had rehearsed in therapy several times. This is what she recalls of how that conversation went.

"Mom, when I was a little girl, why didn't you hug me more often? Why didn't you tell me that you loved me? Whenever I would go and stay the night at my girlfriend's house, her mother would come in at night and hug her and squeeze her and stroke her head and tell her she loved her. I was so envious of them."

"But Mom, whenever you came in at night before going to bed, I would wish expectantly for you to hug and kiss me goodnight. I remember even sitting up and extending my arms out and closing my eyes, hoping that you would understand and hug me. But you never did. All you would do was lay my clothes out for the following day. It's like you were more concerned about what other people were thinking and saying than you were about me."

Her mother, with tears filling her eyes, looked at her daughter, and said, *"Oh, my child, didn't you know? Didn't I ever tell you? When I was a little girl, I had to go to school every day wearing dirty, wrinkled clothes. I swore to God, if I should ever have a daughter like you, that would never happen! When I laid your clothes out each night, that was my way of hugging you. That was my way of saying I love you. Didn't you know?"*

They held each other for the longest time. Longer than ever before. The daughter let go of her resentment. Her mother learned to say, 'I love you,' and hug her daughter whenever they were together and, she consciously made sure that her granddaughter did as well.

For more than two decades, more than twenty missed Mother's Days, their hurts and disappointment drove an invisible wedge between them. And then truth found them and hope found a new meaning for every holiday thereafter.

In joined hands there is still some token of hope.
In the clenched fists there is none.

—*Victor Hugo*

It was my intention to avoid including my own personal journey with this four-letter word. But this story describes the essence of my understanding of hope.

Hope Disguised

I have two grandsons. At the time of this story, Liam is two and Noah is four. They're brothers and they do everything together. I decided to take them fishing. Taking a two-year-old fishing is an event that only another grandfather can appreciate. For Liam, it meant getting wet. Noah wanted to do some serious fishing. This became easier when Liam discovered the playground nearby and off he went, with my wife trailing behind him.

As Noah and I prepared our poles for fishing, I sat next to Noah and pulled out our carton of worms. Putting a worm on a hook properly is an art and I was about to put worms on our hooks. But I have Parkinson's and this day it decided to raise its ugly head. The tremors became uncontrollable as well as the anxiety that goes with them. No matter how hard I tried, I couldn't come close to getting the bait on our hooks. Tears welled into my eyes as I wanted so much to have this precious time of grandfather and grandson. And now it was all falling down around me.

It was as if Noah was reading my mind. This four-year-old, with the wisdom of one so much older, turned to me and said, *"Popi, please. Take my hand and together we will make your shaking stop. Just take my hand."*

I looked at this child for the longest moment and then reached out and gave him my hand. He held it close to his chest and said, *"Popi, you will be okay."* And, miraculously, I was. Within moments, my tremoring and other Parkinson symptoms abated and, together, we were able to bait our hooks.

I am learning that hope often comes unexpectedly. It's disguised, unrecognizable sometimes, but always through my willingness to be open to the moment.

And now this post-script. Noah would catch the biggest bass I have ever seen caught from this lake. No one around us could believe this four-year-old could catch such a trophy fish.

Liam? He just wanted to hold my hand and go for a walk. A walk he deserved.

*Hope is the companion of power
and mother of success;
for who so hopes strongly
has within him the gift of miracles.*

—*Samuel Smiles*

Bibliography

1. <u>Preface to Romans</u> by Martin Luther, 1522.

2. <u>The Concept of Anxiety</u> by Soren Kirkagaard, 1844. English translation by Walter Lowrie, 1944.

3. <u>Death and the Creative Life</u> by L.M. Goodman, The Springer Series, 1981.

4. <u>I Was a Doctor in Auschwitz</u> by Gisella Perl, Phyllis Lassner, Danny Cohen, Eva Hoffman, Lexington Studies in Jewish Literature, Feb. 28, 2019.

Acknowledgments

I want to begin by acknowledging the many families that came to my aid in giving me permission to share their stories and the stories of someone they had loved and lost. Even after all these years, reaching out to them has caused some to "re-visit" that time in their lives and I am humbled that they would ask me to share in that recall. Grief is a stubborn animal.

I also want to acknowledge the people who have been a part of the classes I have taught. They would listen to these stories and help me to clarify the areas that seemed so clear to me, but to the listener was needing more. I am grateful that they would be lovingly critical.

I am especially grateful to my wife, Carol. She was the first to read and also the one who gave me the time I needed to be alone and carve my notes into a story worth reading. Thank you, Carol.

Lastly, to those "saints" who I sense are surrounding me now as their story is told. I pray that they will forgive me if I erred in any way to the accuracy of their story. But I know they will always be in my cheering section.

About The Author

As a counselor in private practice, Dr. Stephenson provided counseling for more than four hundred children, youths, and adults who had been diagnosed with a life-threatening illness. This counseling would also require grief care to their family members and, at times, the community. He has assisted in the care of two communities that experienced major losses to violence.

He has participated in the development of hospices in San Diego, Seattle, Denver, and Chicago areas. His training includes developing a "death ward" in a hospital in Tijuana, Mexico, as well as developing a team of caregivers to provide end-of-life care to young people.

In addition to his private practice, he has also worked in the public sector and also for a large health insurance company, traveling all over the United States to bring a higher quality of mental health and recovery services to their constituents.

Since his retirement, Dr. Stephenson has written six books, two of them related to his work with the terminally ill. His most recent book, *Sunrises and Sunsets*, was inspired by the Twelve-Step program and is devoted to supporting someone who wants to document the change in their lives.

www.ingramcontent.com/pod-product-compliance
Lightning Source LLC
Chambersburg PA
CBHW021112130626
46554CB00002B/660